Social Studies Curriculum Improvement

Raymond H. Muessig, Editor

Bulletin 55

NATIONAL COUNCIL FOR THE SOCIAL STUDIES

NATIONAL COUNCIL FOR THE SOCIAL STUDIES

Geneva Gay was the Publications Board Coordinator for
Social Studies Curriculum Improvement

Library of Congress Catalog Card Number: 78-50869
ISBN 0-87986-018-9
Copyright © 1978 by the
NATIONAL COUNCIL FOR THE SOCIAL STUDIES
2030 M Street, N.W., Washington, D.C. 20036

About the Editor

Raymond H. Muessig is Professor of Social Studies Education at The Ohio State University in Columbus. He has taught and been involved in curriculum improvement since 1955 as a classroom teacher in public schools in Washington and California and as a full-time or visiting university professor at Toledo, Purdue, Minnesota, Stanford, and Massachusetts. Professor Muessig has also worked with teachers, supervisors, curriculum directors, administrators, and parents in many states as a demonstration teacher, consultant, and speaker. He has edited the 1975 NCSS Yearbook and four Bulletins, contributed two chapters to Yearbooks and three to Bulletins, and written for *Social Education*. He is a former member of the NCSS Board of Directors and Executive Committee.

Foreword

The social studies curriculum continually faces the challenge of revision and renewal. In this field the task of curriculum development is never finished. The intricate tie between social studies education and the constantly changing nature of society and the global condition creates the need for ongoing re-examination of curriculum goals and instructional practices.

Currently, there are many demands for curriculum reform. Such curriculum movements as consumer education, energy education, multiethnic education, law-related education, values education, and global education all have vocal and persistent advocates. For teachers, department chairpersons, and social studies coordinators, these movements raise serious questions about revisions of social studies programs. Which of these reforms should be implemented? Why? How? What inservice programs are needed? These are only a few of the compelling questions faced by those educators who are dedicated to the enhancement of the social competence of young people.

The editor and authors of this bulletin have rendered an important service. They have dealt with major curriculum issues and created a practical guide to bring order out of chaos. At a time when external funds for curriculum development are becoming more elusive, and school districts will have to rely increasingly on their own resources, this publication should be especially useful.

In this bulletin, emphasis is placed on the process of curriculum improvement, rather than on the product; and the central role of the teacher is stressed. The reader is presented with a number of examples of curriculum improvement efforts from which a local district can gain meaningful insights. The role and uses of external consultants are thoughtfully examined. Finally, over a hundred useful resources related to curriculum improvement are listed and annotated.

This bulletin is a significant addition to the array of NCSS publications that address the social studies curriculum. While the

NCSS *Curriculum Guidelines* provide a framework for social studies programs, and a number of yearbooks, other bulletins, and issues of *Social Education* speak to substantive dimensions of reform, this publication is a needed tool to translate the substance of curriculum into effective practices that enhance the education of citizens.

The National Council for the Social Studies is deeply appreciative of the time, effort, and contribution made by editor, Raymond H. Muessig, and by the authors of the five chapters of this bulletin.

Anna S. Ochoa, *President*
National Council for the Social Studies

Introduction

"We register kids whenever they come to our high school, even for just a day or so. The idea, you know, is to get as high a 'body count' as we can to keep up our outside financial support level. But we aren't reporting our actual attendance accurately, honestly. Why, on any given school day now, I may have only 40-80 percent of my registered students in my social studies classes! There must be a lot of things that could be tried to 'turn on' kids to school in general and to help teachers learn to work together to improve the social studies program in particular."

"I think I know as much about curriculum *theory* as most social studies teaching department chairpersons, but I'd like to read something *practical* by somebody or to talk with someone who has worked a long time closely with teachers on down-to-earth curriculum reform. I mean, for instance, should you try to get *all* of the teachers with social studies classes to work on improving the social studies offerings? Should you try to get some district money and just buy lists of objectives or resource units or curriculum guides or published programs, or should you start from scratch and attempt to get teachers to build a whole social studies curriculum from the ground up? If you can get funds for outside help, should you use just one consultant from the beginning to the end of a curriculum revision effort, or should you bring in a group of people to help? Do you understand the kinds of things that I'd like to know?"

"The three of us were at this elementary school the day it opened its doors in 1954. We were new teachers, and were we ever fired up! They needed teachers *then* and actually *recruited* us through the university placement service. We had a lot of kids to teach. Our school levies passed. Additional teachers were hired because of growth and employment mobility, and we came into contact with lots of good, different ideas. There was money for teaching materials and released time and substitutes, so we could work closely and continuously together on the social studies program and other related areas and fire up each other. It was a gas! Then . . . well . . . I don't know. We lost our momentum. Frankly, I don't think I've had a new idea or tried anything really creative for four or five years. We've got to have some outside help, some fresh things to read, some contacts with teachers and proposals in other school districts, some time for personal and professional renewal. That's it: *renewal!*"

"We've had two sessions with that new, young consultant . . . from some social studies project in the East, I think. . . . Anyway, the central administration intends to use the guy to help us with the revision of our social studies program. He's smart enough, I guess. And he's certainly got a lot of drive. But he isn't dry behind the ears! A number of his ideas may be new to him, but we knew them by other names years ago and tried them out and discarded or modified them for sound reasons. He ought to do substantial reading in the concrete social studies publications—as we do now and have done for a long time—get more of a sense of some of the levelheaded, worldly-wise history of social studies curriculum development, and ponder things written by some seasoned consultants. Should we go to him on the side with some advice or give the supervisor the word?"

Statements and questions such as those above may be heard today in many parts of our nation in dialogues among elementary and secondary social studies classroom teachers in hallways and lounges, in building and district curriculum committee sessions, in faculty meetings, in university graduate seminars, and in local, state, regional, and national conferences involving dedicated people who are on the "firing line" daily.

Social Studies Curriculum Improvement: A Guide for Local Committees, published by the National Council for the Social Studies in 1965, was sufficiently well received that some kind of replacement was deemed appropriate by the Publications Board. However, there have been so many developments during the intervening years—such as those suggested by the quotations above—that a completely new Bulletin, enlarged in its scope, was required, instead of just a revision. It is hoped that this 1978 offering will be even more useful than was its predecessor.

Individual members of the National Council for the Social Studies, representatives of NCSS committees, chapter authors, and others have tried to keep the needs of various potential audiences in mind during the creation, writing, and editing of this Bulletin. *Social Studies Curriculum Improvement* was designed first and foremost for practicing classroom teachers engaged in actual curriculum work; but the people who work closely with teachers in school districts—resource teachers, principals, supervisors, curriculum directors. superintendents, and their assistants—were kept in mind as well, as the project evolved. Also those who educate teachers and administrators and who serve as curriculum consultants figured prominently in the planning and execution of this publication. It was hoped, too, that some parents, school board members, legislators, and citizens in general might become members of the reading group. In short, this publication tries to provide varied insights for a diverse, large population whose members care about the social education of our nation's most precious resource: children and youth.

This brief publication will not become a "classic" in the history of educational thought. If it enjoys any immortality, it will be a functional, not a literary, one, as it directs and inspires teachers who, in turn, touch the lives of learners. The authors include competent, experienced scholars, theorists, researchers, administrators, and teachers; and they have chosen an open, upfront position over the safety of a remote ivory tower. A better tomorrow for the social studies is envisioned in much of what is said here, but this is not a view of a Utopian scheme for the year 2500 A.D. Nor is it offered as a panacea developed by persons with a one-track commitment that they share among themselves or expect others to embrace without question or reflection. The National Council for the Social Studies is a heterogeneous organization in which pluralism is not an abstraction but a concrete reality. The authors of this Bulletin, therefore, have been encouraged to express their own points of view, not to adhere to any kind of official party line. Some statements which may appear as inconsistencies from chapter to chapter represent, instead, honest disagreement.

In Chapter I, "Some Thoughts on Curriculum Improvement," Raymond H. Muessig shares impressions formed in over two decades of varied professional work. He develops the ideas that the process of curriculum improvement is more important than the product, that the teacher is the key person in all stages of curricular reform, that there are a number of important drawbacks associated with trying to involve all classroom teachers in curriculum work, that a single theory of social studies education need not be followed, and that there are few "bargain prices" in curricular undertakings. Muessig provides abundant examples, which should be read carefully, as they have been included to clarify and amplify key points. He concludes with ten ways that people involved in curriculum improvement can judge the extent to which they have been successful.

Early in the planning of this Bulletin, a series of thoughts seemed to converge: (1) There was a desire to have some material reporting and analyzing actual curriculum improvement in one local school district. (2) There was a feeling that a more typical, less publicized, heterogeneous, city system should be found, instead of a wealthy, well publicized, homogenous, suburban district. (3) There was a belief that more "credible" copy might be written by actual school district participants than by some outside project consultant or university consultant. Chapter II, "Social Studies Curriculum Improvement Efforts in the Mansfield City Schools: 1960–1977," has been developed along the lines just enumerated. Together, John F. Cunningham, Director of Instruction, Judy Fox, a teacher at Johnny Appleseed Junior High School, and Lowell T. Smith, Director of Personnel and Supervisor of Social Studies, represent educators with over sixty years of public school experience; and all three have more than "paid their dues" in social studies curriculum work. Cunningham, in order of service, has been a secondary teacher, an elementary teacher, an elementary principal, and a curriculum director. Fox has been an elementary teacher, an elementary social studies resource teacher, and a junior high school social studies teacher. Smith has been a senior high school social studies teacher, an assistant principal, and a personnel director and a supervisor of social studies. Chapter II begins with a brief discussion of some of the social studies curriculum problems which existed in Mansfield in the early 1960s and the start of limited reforms. It then touches on topics such as: improvements attempted over the ensuing years, viewpoints—pro and con—on approaches employed, insights gained and applicable to future efforts, programs for inservice education purposes, tasks accomplished through released time and summer employment, sources and uses made of outside funding, examples of possibilities gained from other projects and perceptions shared with others, contributions made by outside consultants, opportunities taken to secure broader community involvement, illustrations of objectives and resource units developed, procedures learned in social studies curriculum work of benefit to other program areas, and uses of local moneys to continue undertakings supported initially by outside grants.

Jo Ann Cutler Sweeney and Gloria Contreras, both social studies educators at The University of Texas at Austin, have contributed this Bulletin's third chapter, "Curriculum Improvement: A Sampler of Noteworthy Experiences." In various parts of this publication, curriculum workers are reminded that they need not reinvent the wheel. They can profit from the varied experiences of others, at different levels and locations, inside and outside of social studies education. Sweeney and Contreras review curriculum changes in social studies programs, in cross-disciplinary projects, and in generic prototypes. Examples include the West Islip Public Schools Program, the Social Studies Field Agent Training Program, the Twin Cities Social Studies Service Center, the Development Economic Education Program, the Foxfire Project, the Mendocino College Interdisciplinary Education Project, the Adult Performance Level Project, the Peoria and the World Project, the Esperanza Model, the Parent Involvement component of the project Follow Through, and the Urban-Rural Development Program. Chapter III offers frequent, brief summaries of what can be learned from the illustrations, and it concludes with some general observations.

During the development stages of this Bulletin, there was widespread agreement on the need to include material concerned with locating and using various forms of assistance in curriculum improvement. Nancy W. Bauer, an experienced and noted curriculum designer and consultant, was asked to deal with concerns in this area. In Chapter IV, Bauer asserts that today social studies people must further tap their strengths and find out ways to get even more out of the scarce dollars they invest in curriculum improvement, and that it is desirable to look at those who use consultants and to examine the consultants themselves. She treats some of the appeals and drawbacks associated with the utilization of such outsiders as subject-matter specialists, those skilled in application, other practitioners, supervisors, teachers, state-wide supervisors, and publishers' representatives. Bauer says that outsiders are used most effectively when a school district prepares carefully to select and to involve a consultant wisely, when there is agreement among parents, educators, and political leaders regarding those needs of learners which should be met, when perceived needs are compared with research, when common questions have been framed before the consultant's appearance, when district leaders are trained along with the staff, and when there is a plan for implementing the results of district deliberations.

Chapter IV does not ignore the use of insiders, however. After a school system has a sense of direction, an adopted philosophy and policy, and the necessary materials, "home" people can be used alone or in concert with outside consultants. Insiders are aware of details and limitations and able to share their insights as colleagues.

Following a discussion of the need for a support system which can translate good ideas into sound practices that have a chance to survive, this chapter concerns itself with important qualifications which consultants must possess or acquire, and questions which consultants should ask themselves and mottoes they should recall in order to increase their contributions.

Bauer concludes her chapter with the observation that optimistic realists with a sense of humor are needed to improve the human condition through the development of competent and humane children.

Jack W. Miller's final chapter, "Additional Sources of Materials for Curriculum Workers and Teachers," in *Social Studies Curriculum Improvement: A Guide for Local Committees* (1965), was praised so highly by reviewers and subsequently by other readers over the years that he was among the very first authors identified for this new Bulletin. Miller, Professor of Education and Director, Advanced Graduate Programs for Curriculum Leadership Personnel, George Peabody College for Teachers, was joined by Edward V. Johnson, a Peabody Doctoral Research Assistant, in the preparation of Chapter V, "Library Resources To Support Curriculum Improvement," which serves as a valuable conclusion to this publication.

Miller and Johnson have written readable and insightful annotations for well over 100 resources related to diverse, yet interrelated, topics, such as preparing for curriculum improvement in general and in the social studies in particular; curricular evaluation; theories of instruction; goals; scope and sequence considerations; aids to curriculum building; curriculum guides; instructional media for teachers; and social studies projects. Surely curriculum workers will refer to this chapter for years to come.

Raymond H. Muessig, *Editor*

Contents

1

Some Thoughts on Curriculum Improvement

Raymond H. Muessig

Introduction

A half-century ago, Robert Benchley wrote a witty little essay called "What College Did to Me," which has often been quoted and adapted by authors up to the present. The following statements—appearing in a random and partial manner—are just a few of the "profound" perceptions which the American humorist lists as having resulted from his higher education:

> *Nine-tenths of the girls in a girls' college are not pretty.*
> *You can sleep undetected in a lecture course by resting the head on the hand as if shading the eyes.*
> *You needn't be fully dressed if you wear a cap and gown to nine o'clock recitation.*
> *Powder rubbed on the chin will take the place of a shave if the room isn't very light.*
> *A sock with a hole in the toe can be worn inside out with comparative comfort.*
> *You can get dressed much quicker in the morning if the night before when you are going to bed you take off your trousers and underdrawers at once, leaving the latter inside the former.*[1]

Perhaps this chapter should have been entitled "What Curriculum Improvement Did to Me," for I am going to use a per-

---

RAYMOND H. MUESSIG is Professor of Social Studies Education, Faculty of Humanities Education, College of Education, The Ohio State University, Columbus, Ohio.

1

sonal, informal, experiential format slightly reminiscent of Benchley's. I, too, have decided to share some impressions on things I believe I have learned over a period of more than twenty years. As a classroom teacher in two states, I served from 1955–57 as the chairperson of a grade-level curriculum committee for a school district and wrote portions of a new social studies guide. As a professor, my responsibilities during school years and summer sessions in six universities have included teaching undergraduate and graduate courses in general curriculum and in social studies curriculum, and guiding the independent study of teachers, supervisors, and curriculum directors at work on programs. As a consultant, I have engaged in social studies curriculum study, revision, design, development, and implementation with teachers and others in almost half of the states, usually on a K-12 basis and occasionally over a period of years in the same school district.

The thoughts expressed here, then, are based on certain kinds of experiences which have led me to draw conclusions that might have been different had I faced other circumstances. Suffice it to say that competent, responsible curriculum workers could disagree with my observations for sound reasons.

Item: In Figment County there are three school districts,* each of which has a central administration building with a similar marble portal over which the name of the system is carved in large capital letters; under the name, there is a saying in smaller capital and lower case letters below. Approaching the first entryway, one sees the words *MUNIFICENT HEIGHTS SUBURBAN SCHOOLS*, under which appears *"No hay limites para la ambición."—Cervantes* (roughly translated as "The sky's the limit."). Munificent has maximal support for everything educational, including all curricular endeavors. On the opposite side of the county, across the railroad tracks, one reads the name *PARSIMONIOUS BOTTOMS LOCAL SCHOOL DISTRICT*, and below it *"Lasciate ogni speranza, voi ch'entrate."—Dante* (or "Abandon hope, all ye who enter here."). Parsimonious has lost two tax levies in a row and cannot even replace decrepit textbooks, let alone consider conservative revisions (not to mention daring innovations) in curriculum. In the center of Figment County, one observes the name *THRIFTY PLAINS CITY*

---

*The names of all schools and individuals referred to in "Items" are fictitious. Any similarities with the names of real schools and individuals are accidental.

SCHOOLS above *"Wir tun das Beste, was wir können."*—*Kopf-schmerzen* ("We do the best we can with what we have."). With its modest budget, Thrifty cannot do anything sweeping or exciting, but it can make a curricular repair or modification or addition here or there from time to time.

Most of the ideas which follow could be placed on a scale ranging somewhere between Munificent and Thrifty. The order in which perceptions appear is anything but sacred, as the most significant consideration one time may be less crucial in another context. Many of the elements are interrelated and could be combined in various ways.

A List of Points
Related to Curriculum Improvement

1. *The process of curriculum improvement is more important than the product.* Curriculum guides, resource units, scope and sequence foldout charts, annotated catalogs of books and other sources recommended for teachers and of multimedia instructional materials suggested for learners and publications for parents and the general public—all these are necessary and helpful. However, one of the best of many appealing features of curriculum reform is what it can do *to* and *for* the participants. Curricular activities provide excellent opportunities for those involved to think through what they are and should be doing and to arrive at mindful, clear, defensible, consistent, solid bases for making many isolated decisions; to interact purposefully and amiably with colleagues and others, both lay and professional; to translate into concrete practice some of the otherwise rather abstract theory encountered in university, college, and inservice courses, professional literature, and local, state, regional, and national social studies conferences; to uncover individual and shared difficulties and shortcomings which can then be overcome by continuous informal and formal study (e.g., university seminars formed around teachers' actual requests); and to concentrate their efforts, to see a resource unit or other educational devices all of the way through from beginning to end without the usual distractions experienced most days in schools. Additionally, it should be noted that an emphasis on process recognizes that curriculum improvement should be a *continuous* effort, rather than a job terminating in a *finished* product.

2. *The classroom teacher is the alpha and omega of curriculum improvement*. There are many components in a good social studies program, obviously; but the teacher is the best person to initiate specific reforms, to continue particular improvements, and to make given refinements work with pupils. The most genuine, significant, functional, and enduring curriculum improvement begins from within an individual teacher who is acutely aware of and who wants seriously to do something about needs, interests, problems, and aspirations suggested by (1) the nature and course of past, present, and future society at all levels, ranging from the interpersonal on through the global; (2) the growth, development, and potential of children and youth; (3) the attributes, purposes, tools, techniques, and content of history and the social sciences; (4) theories of social studies education; and (5) his or her own personal and professional characteristics and capacities.

Individual teachers who share mutual frustrations, desires, proposals, and goals; who voluntarily pool their intelligence, knowledge, abilities, creativity, and energies; and who are supported well by the necessary resources can just about perform curricular miracles. However, changes forced upon teachers alone or in various kinds of groups by students, parents, school boards, special interest groups, legislatures, resource teachers, department chairpersons, principals, supervisors, curriculum directors, superintendents, consultants, project developers, *ad infinitum*—through coercion, law, fiat, indoctrination, inculcation, manipulation, or other means—are less likely to take root and to flourish than those each teacher really wants for herself or himself and for her or his pupils. If teachers' dignity, integrity, individuality, diversity, open expression of contrasting ideas, and experimentation with myriad perspectives, objectives, offerings, methods, materials, and evaluative procedures cannot be maintained today and expanded tomorrow, there is a very real possibility that teaching will become more and more of a boring, automated, slavish, day-to-day chore and less and less of a unique, bold, stimulating, lifelong quest.

3. *Although ideally it might seem like a good idea to involve every social studies teacher in curriculum improvement, realistically 100% participation can have its drawbacks*. Below are some arguments for and against trying to include in curricular undertakings all of those who teach something in the social stud-

ies area in a school district. Although I can think of more cons than pros, this does not mean that each assertion has equal weight.

Arguments for Involving Everyone

- A person strongly committed to popular sovereignty could posit that all people affected by a decision should participate in the making of that decision. If all the social studies teachers are involved in a grassroots fashion at every stage in curriculum reform, they will understand a revised or new program better, offer less resistance to changes, and work harder to make implementation a success.
- Curriculum work is an important learning experience which every teacher must have as a part of his or her inservice education. Teachers must be brought along continuously if they are key components in curriculum betterment.
- In groups where people interact, the whole (the outcome of sharing many different and gradually better ideas) can be greater than the sum of its individual parts (the actual number of participants). By getting all of the teachers of social studies—with variations in their place of birth and/or growth and development, age, sex, race, ethnic group, education, experience, field of substantive specialization, and grade level assignment—to labor together, the result could be a richer, more realistic, better balanced curriculum and an increasingly cooperative total social studies faculty throughout the school district.
- Since all social studies teachers can benefit directly or indirectly from improvements made in the curriculum, everyone should do her or his share.

Arguments Against Involving Everyone

- Some teachers fear any kind of change, resist efforts to encourage and help them move away from the use of a single textbook or some other ingrained approach, and, if asked to serve on committees, detract from the efforts of others who see a need to bring about various reforms.
- Curriculum improvement is hard work, and there are teachers who cannot or do not want to expend that kind of energy.
- Regardless of stimulating activities which may surround them, certain individuals are too unimaginative to catch—let alone to generate—fresh ideas.

- Writing is a complex, demanding art, and some teachers cannot organize and express thoughts well enough to produce usable materials.
- Curricular endeavors often put people very closely together for days and weeks, and not everyone has the human relations skills, tolerance, patience, and sense of humor necessary to bolster joint morale and achievement.
- There are many teachers who do not assign top priority to social studies, even though they have instructional responsibilities in that arena, and who prefer to do other kinds of curriculum construction. This group would include some of those who teach in self-contained elementary classrooms where numerous subject fields are involved and where an individual may have less academic preparation, interest, and competence in social studies than in such areas as language arts, arithmetic, science, health, industrial arts, music, or art. Also there are junior high school people with core or block-time schedules (e.g., English *and* social studies) and persons in smaller senior high schools with mixed loads of two or three subjects (English, Spanish, physical education, health, driver education, etc.) who may have college *minors* in history and/or just one of the social sciences. At any rate, no one should be dragged kicking and screaming into social studies program development.
- From the vantage point of many experienced social studies supervisors, curriculum directors, and consultants, it is more productive, economical, and enjoyable to work with 1-10 teachers who care and who really "have it" than it is to try to accommodate 30-60 persons who would rather be doing almost anything else. Curriculum improvement does not have to be an all-fronts, full-scale attack all of the time. It can be as humble—though nonetheless important—as a single teacher or a small group of professionals with an idea worth developing.

Item: It is early spring in a city of moderate size. Quite a number of people—including parents, secondary students, management and labor spokespersons, two school board members, and five social studies teachers in two high schools—have revealed in various ways a sincere interest in "doing something about consumer education." Further, the director of secondary education (fortunately, a former outstanding social studies teacher) cares about the expressed concerns of others, decides to do what she can, seeks financial support in the community, and eventually secures rather generous contributions from a local of a union and from a businesspersons' association.

The scene is set for limited curricular effort, with sufficient money to pay two of the most able and enthusiastic social studies teachers for just two weeks at the beginning of the summer to build a fairly comprehensive resource unit with the assistance of an outside consultant. The remaining resources are used to purchase certain carefully chosen instructional materials, which are assembled in the form of a portable kit for the use of one teacher at a time. Additionally, six teacher volunteers (including the unit writers)—two in autumn, two in winter, and two in spring—working with some twelfth-grade classes where time can be allotted for experimental electives, agree to try out the unit and to write criticisms and suggestions for improvements directly on copies of the unit as they teach it.

Representatives of the sponsors and others who are interested in consumer education are invited to visit the classes. Articles are written for the local newspaper, and photographs of class activities are included. Funds from other sources are solicited and obtained, and plans are made for unit revision and amplification and for inservice education for a wider circle of motivated teachers, again involving the consultant. An awareness of this success story encourages three other teachers to use *Teaching About Women in the Social Studies: Concepts, Methods, and Materials*, edited by Jean Dresden Grambs and published by the National Council for the Social Studies, to begin a serious study of ways that sexism might be eliminated in their own social studies classes, and of ways in which they might, in time, meaningfully involve colleagues in this endeavor.

- Finally—let us all be grateful—there exist those loving, inventive, animated teachers who—in spite of shouts of "Heresy!" from certain curriculum theorists, school administrators, and others—should be left alone to delight in each wonderful day with their lucky charges and should be freed from everything possible which interferes with their spontaneous artistry and saps their physical and psychic strength. One might assume that these "teacher stars" would make excellent curriculum workers, but I have not found this to be the case. First, they are usually "Lone Eagles" who think, create, and act best on their own, not in committees. Second, unlike many professional associates, they do not look forward to released time for district or school curriculum reform, for this means being away from *their* beloved pupils and "handing the children over to all kinds of substitutes" who might damage the carefully established classroom climate. Third, these virtuosi seldom write down a great deal. They are "naturals" who "play it by ear" and can turn many unplanned, emergent class needs and interests into glorious, teachable moments. Making them sit down and grind out such things as endless behavioral objectives is a sure way to reduce their effectiveness.

4. *A single theory of social studies education (e.g., subject-centered, citizenship, emergent needs, social functions, reflective, structure of the disciplines, informal, moral) need not be followed by an entire school district (K-12), by a whole school (primary, intermediate, elementary, middle, open, junior high, senior high), by all of the teachers at the same grade level (third, sixth, ninth, twelfth), or even by a given teacher throughout a school year.* Although there could still be an occasional purist who might object to this point, most of the people who have lived through various proposals, experiments, projects, debates, fads, and annual "Madison Avenue" kinds of "buzz words" have come to realize that social studies education is a complex, eclectic, protean, and sometimes amorphous field with considerable overlapping and slippage with respect to theories.

Item: The Excelsior Public Schools in the State of Flux (where a K-12 social studies program is strongly recommended but where no specific course titles have been mandated by the State Legislature, Board of Education, etc.), are situated in a rather large city with a heterogeneous and mobile population. People from different racial, religious, and ethnic groups live amicably in various parts of Excelsior. Through press releases, newsletters, speeches at district in-service conferences, visits to building faculty meetings, participation in curriculum committee sessions, conversations with individual teachers after classroom observations, and personal notes to teachers, principals, and supervisors, the Superintendent of Schools has encouraged all of the teachers in general and the social studies teachers in particular to do everything possible to foster humane interpersonal and intergroup relations, to individualize and personalize instruction, to increase open educational opportunity for all learners, and to provide greater variety and more alternatives in schooling.

Driving to all of Excelsior's schools, it has become evident to the Supervisor of Elementary Social Studies and to the Supervisor of Secondary Social Studies that the Superintendent of Schools has inspired many teachers. For example, three teachers with ninth-grade social studies classes at a junior high school have begun sharing their concerns about preparing their students for the variegated demands of high school social studies. They have pooled their talents and developed three sets of five shoeboxes containing hundreds of 4″ × 6″ cards. On each card, the teachers have written one unique, meaningful, appealing learning activity which may serve reinforcement, diagnostic, remedial, or enrichment purposes. The cards have been ordered in each box so the activities go from easy to difficult, concrete to abstract, at various taxonomic levels. During times that are available for independent study, students may start at any point in one or more of the boxes; and they are challenged eventually to progress at individual rates as far as possible in all five boxes. One shoebox contains subject-centered cards and brings learners into contact with important new content and helps them to master and to transfer significant substance that has been or is being learned. Another container focuses on citizenship activities, including possibilities for getting involved in civic projects. A third box concentrates on key concepts and generalizations from history and the social sciences, discovered to a considerable extent through creative inquiry strategies. Still another shoebox holds vital personal-social reflective issues which stimulate class members to clarify their values. The fifth box deals directly with many special and all-purpose skills related to history and the social sciences and to different theories of social studies education. The three teachers plan to involve their students continuously in an evaluation of the activities appearing on the cards and to remove unsuccessful ideas, to clarify and to amplify certain approaches, and to add new suggestions.

The Principal of Jane Addams Elementary School is a master teacher, often found in K-6 classrooms throughout the school. He believes in supportive, invitational supervision, pitching in to help teachers whenever they request assistance. As a principal, he feels that teachers need maximal autonomy in order to grow personally and professionally. He thinks that teachers should have as much latitude as possible—especially with respect to the theories to which they adhere—as long as they "care about kids, know *why* they are doing *what* they are doing, work their heads off, and get through to children." Knowing the preceding about him, it should not be surprising that some of the best teachers at Addams Elementary are a study in theoretical diversity. For instance, Helen K., the top kindergarten teacher, has been spurred by the Superintendent's efforts and has renewed her commitment to a kind of "Progressive" philosophy of social studies education. She has said to the Principal that part of her view of " '*social* studies' includes the use of play as a *socializing* mechanism by which a child can move gradually from just a 'me-centered' view of the world to a concern for the needs of others as well." Bill C., Addams' finest second grade teacher, used the entire summer of 1974 to observe classes in British primary schools in many parts of England. During the 1975–76 school year, he took a professional leave to complete a master's degree in early and middle childhood education, which included special areas in social studies education and informal-open education. Bill C. is so skilled in interpreting an integrated-day philosophy that he does not try to distinguish where " 'social studies' begins and ends." He is uncomfortable with the idea of a social studies program planned and set down on paper by one or more teachers *before* children even arrive at school. Rather, he likes to identify the needs and interests of his own pupils and *then* to blend tailor-made learning experiences from a number of compatible subject areas around the children. However, Ian D., a highly-regarded fourth grade teacher, believes in teaching "social studies" as such, in extensive *pre*-planning to assure the inclusion of essential content for the entire class and to avoid needless overlapping, in an expanding circles scope and sequence pattern with themes ("transportation," "communication," etc.) interwoven around a year of "Our State," and in accommodating special needs and interests through individual and committee projects. Babette A., the best sixth grade teacher at Addams Elementary, utilizes "The Western Hemisphere" to develop overall geographic understandings (including concepts and generalizations that are both introduced and revisited as opportunities arise) and specific map skills necessary for junior high school and other aspects of life.

Fred K. has taught various social studies subjects and grades at the secondary level for seventeen years. At present, he has five eleventh-grade American history classes at Meriwether Lewis High School. Although he does not agree with the policy, there is "homogeneous grouping" at Lewis; and he has the "11-1's," "11-3's," "11-6's," "11-8's," and "11-15's," Fred K. has always thought of himself as a "pragmatic" teacher who "uses anything that works with students." He has kept up pretty well in social studies education over the years, pondered and experimented with different theories, and become quite eclectic. Since almost all of his "11-1's" and "11-2's" have expressed a serious interest in higher education and have asked for help in preparing for college entrance examinations and in getting ready for university course work, he relies heavily on the subject-centered *and* the structure of the disciplines theories of social studies education. He tries to make the names, dates, places, and events likely to appear in standardized tests interesting and easy to recall; *and* he surveys history and the social sciences, touching upon the nature and development of those fields, representative concepts and generalizations, basic tools and techniques, and exemplary literature. With the "11-6's" and "11-8's," Fred K.

often turns to a kind of reflective approach, in which he teaches learners to uncover and to use relevant data, concepts, generalizations, and skills necessary to warrant beliefs associated with controversial issues. Finally, with members of his "11-15" class, he uses a form of citizenship education theory, as he understands it. Using a multimedia approach, he familiarizes students with American history, ideals, government, economics, society, and culture. He encourages thoughtful discussions about civic rights, responsibilities, and opportunities; and he relates some of the things being learned in the social studies class to the school's career education program, paying particular attention to occupational trends in the United States.

Thus, it is apparent that a single theory of social studies education is not being followed in the Excelsior Public Schools, and that—apropos of the fourth point—a mixture of philosophies would often be encountered in many school districts.

5. *There are few "bargain prices" in curriculum improvement.* School districts which expect to get "something for nothing" are almost always disappointed with the curricular results. As with so many areas of life, the more that is invested in an endeavor, the more that may be gained from the expenditure. Below are three composite items based upon real situations. The first case provides a negative example against which the remaining two more positive instances might be compared.

Item: The people in the central administration office of the Crab Grass Public Schools wanted "a 'new' social studies guide with 'behavioral objectives,' " largely to satisfy a strong suggestion made by a recent visiting inspection team dispatched by the State Department of Instruction. The only money provided for this undertaking was for the mimeographing of copies of the guide, which the K-12 social studies teachers themselves were even expected to type, collate, and staple. Each building principal was required to assign one teacher to the project, and the teachers named were told to meet in an elementary school cafeteria every Wednesday from 3:45–5:30 P.M., after a full day in the classroom. Discovering that they would have no consultative help from the central office or the outside and that no one really seemed to care about the quality of the guide, the teachers worked out the least time-consuming system which occurred to them. They figured out the minimally requisite headings and their respective pages of copy, divided the sum of the necessary pages by the number of participants, and agreed to write, as quickly as possible, the same number of pages. Nothing was said about overlapping, continuity, editing, or proofreading. The teachers seemed to be progressing well until they realized how trying, tiring, boring, and time-consuming it was to write one behavioral objective after another. However, one resourceful old pedagogue located a classified advertisement at the back of a professional journal which promised a long list of social studies behavioral objectives for a nominal fee, a list that became even more manageable when divided among the entire group. Other than by the unfortunate individual who had to retype the commercial list for reproduction purposes, the behavioral objectives were never read. The guide to the district's social studies curriculum was turned out in record time, placed in the central office files, and distributed to every social studies teacher, who placed it in the bottom righthand drawer of his or her desk, where it remained untouched.

Item: Almost a week before the start of a school year, the Lilac Suburban School District included selected K-12 social studies teachers, representative principals, a prominent speaker, outstanding demonstration teachers from four different school systems, two eminent university consultants, an assistant superintendent in charge of curriculum and instruction, the superintendent, two school board members, and four parents in a three-day retreat held at a beautifully wooded place. Everyone rose early and worked hard into the evening on social studies curriculum reform. Small groups—arranged at first horizontally along grade-level lines and later vertically from K-12 to improve the flow of a proposed scope and sequence pattern—convened in rooms in the main lodge and in cabins, and the superintendent moved from group to group and contributed as much as anyone in the relaxed, open exchanges. The last night, the total-group summary session was held in a friendly atmosphere around a fire in the massive stone fireplace in the living room of the lodge. Everyone was deeply impressed and inspired by what was accomplished—both in terms of the excellent ideas recorded and the obvious advances in human relations—and the school board members and parents were among the first to say that the funds used for the retreat had been employed wisely.

Item: The Azalea City Schools pledged themselves (in advance each year for three years) to set aside adequate funds for serious social studies curriculum development. Money was earmarked for released time during instructional days and for full-time employment a week at a time during breaks between school terms and school years; for consultants; for visits to enlightened school districts, project centers, and universities; for attendance at state, regional, and national social studies conferences; for the purchase of reproduced resource units and curriculum guides; and for fairly abundant instructional materials necessary to launch units and to sustain those units during and after their completion. Although many theoreticians insist that teachers must devote considerable time to framing an "original" credo and a seemingly related inventory of overall and immediate aims, the Azalea City Schools "fudged a bit" and did things in a somewhat "backward" manner. Deciding to initiate the curriculum improvement process with a thorough investigation of available instructional materials, the district committee requested transportation and expenses for one elementary teacher and one secondary teacher to attend a forthcoming Annual Meeting of the National Council for the Social Studies. Although it meant giving up numerous interesting and worthwhile area tours, school visitations, clinics, committee and section meetings, and general sessions, the two elected teachers concentrated on those possibilities germane to educational media. Going carefully through the convention program, the Azalea teachers divided two evenings of film showings, the morning and afternoon open meetings of the Instructional Media and the Curriculum Advisory Committees, respectively, and four especially relevant section meetings. In addition, they counted the number of companies found in the "Directory of Exhibitors" toward the back of the convention program; split that number; visited each booth; filled four free shopping bags with promotional literature; requested that examination copies of textbooks and preview prints of films and filmstrips be sent to the Azalea City Schools; and invited firms to contact the district regarding the possibility of scheduling the visits of sales representatives, consultants, designers, and authors to present textbook series, programs, multimedia kits, maps and globes, paperback collections, current events periodicals, simulations and games, and models to Azalea's social studies curriculum workers.

The elementary and secondary teachers formed into the Azalea City Schools Social Studies Curriculum Committee had a marvelous time examining and evaluating educational media and even trying out instructional materials in some of their classes; and they became members of an eager, well informed, cohesive team. Using their thorough knowledge of the best teaching resources available (and which the district indicated it could and would purchase), the teachers took a fresh look at the needs, interests, and abilities of Azalea's students, at relevant content, at appropriate methods, and at suitable evaluative procedures. *Then*, they jointly drafted and refined a limited selection of the most pointed, personalized, practical, defensible, articulated, and cumulative objectives the school system had ever seen. The remainder of the curriculum development went so well that the overall design, the K-12 guide, and all of the basic resource units at each grade level were completed in the late fall of the third year.

Since allocated funds had been used wisely all along the way and conserved by an earlier conclusion than had been anticipated, the delighted central administration and the school board were persuaded by the chief university consultant to reward and to encourage further the hard working, cooperative, spirited, efficient Committee members. The consultant said that the participants were really on top of educational media, and he recommended that each social studies curriculum worker be budgeted up to $600 the remainder of the school year for personal selections, through the district purchasing office, of instructional materials that would enrich the individual's classroom teaching. After considerable discussion, the allotment agreed on was $350.

Fairly soon thereafter, Azalea's English teachers requested funds for major curriculum reform.

Conclusion

Having introduced this chapter with a bit of Robert Benchley's humor, I have decided to conclude with a few words from Benchley's "Easy Tests," followed by some "easy tests" of my own.

> *One of the measures suggested to aid in the reduction of the number of automobile accidents is the prohibition of gasoline sales to intoxicated drivers. . . .*
> *The trouble with the gas prohibition is that the gas-station man is to be the judge of who is intoxicated and who isn't. . . .*
>
>   *. . .*
>
> *For the aid of the gas-station boys we might list a few infallible symptoms of intoxication in drivers:*
> *1. When the driver is sitting with his back against the instrument board and his feet on the driver's seat.*
>
>   *. . .*
>
> *4. When the driver points to the gas-tank and says, "A pound of liver, please."*
> *5. When the driver is in fancy dress with a paper whistle in his mouth which he is blowing constantly.*
> *6. If the driver insists that the gas-station man take the driver's seat while he (the driver) fills the tank, first exchanging hats.*[2]

For the consideration of people engaged in social studies curriculum improvement, we might list a few infallible symptoms of success:

1. When the educational experiences of children and youth have been enriched because their teachers engaged in curriculum work.
2. When all of the curriculum workers have grown personally and professionally as a result of their participation.
3. When teachers are involved in curriculum improvement because they want to be.
4. When teachers who did not want to participate initially in a curriculum project decide that something worthwhile is taking place and that they should become involved.
5. When curriculum improvement becomes a continuous process, rather than an occasional, short-lived effort.
6. When teachers, wishing continuous social studies curriculum reform, persist in requesting funds for outside consultants, expenses to attend conferences, university graduate study, released time during the school year, summer employment, professional publications, instructional materials, etc.
7. When teachers know better than ever before *why* they are doing *what* they are doing in the classroom.
8. When teachers spark each other informally by trading their best ideas in personal discussions, by observing and critiquing each other in their respective classrooms, by exchanging materials and written suggestions all over the school district, etc.
9. When district-developed social studies curriculum guides and resource units are seen on top of teachers' desks and are really *used* frequently, instead of being filed.
10. When channels of communication are opened and strengthened throughout the district, and students, parents, teachers, principals, supervisors, curriculum directors, chief administrators, school board members, and the general public all talk and listen more to each other and like better what they say and hear.

Footnotes

[1]Excerpts from "What College Did to Me," in *The Early Worm* by Robert Benchley. Copyright © 1927 by Harper & Brothers. Published by Blue Ribbon Books. Used by permission of Harper & Row, Publishers.

[2]Excerpts from "Easy Tests," in *The Benchley Roundup* by Nathaniel Benchley. Copyright © 1954 by Nathaniel Benchley. Published by Harper Colophon Books, 1976. Used by permission of Harper & Row, Publishers.

2

Social Studies Curriculum Improvement in the Mansfield City Schools: 1960-1977

John F. Cunningham, Judy Fox, and Lowell T. Smith

Mansfield, Ohio, a city of 55,047 population, is located in the north-central part of the state. Currently, the population composition, with many nationalities and ethnic groups represented, is almost 85% white and 15% minority.

The city has a diversity of industry whose products range from snowmobiles to hair dryers, and from household appliances to heavy steel. Many of the industries, such as the Tappan Company and the Ohio Brass Company, were founded by local industrial pioneers.

The community offers many educational opportunities from kindergarten to technical university training. Likewise, cultural facilities and programs—such as Bromfield's Malabar Farm, Kingwood Horticultural Center, the Fine Arts Guild, the symphony orchestra, and two little-theatre groups—meet various interests and needs of its population.

JOHN F. CUNNINGHAM is Director of Instruction, Mansfield City Schools, Mansfield, Ohio. JUDY FOX is a teacher at Johnny Appleseed Junior High School, Mansfield City Schools, Mansfield, Ohio. LOWELL T. SMITH is Director of Personnel and Supervisor of Social Studies, Mansfield City Schools, Mansfield, Ohio.

While the city is not large, it still has experienced many of the problems which prevail in large cities.

PHASE I: 1960–1964

During the early 1960s a number of teachers and administrators in the Mansfield City Schools were becoming aware of the fact that the existing social studies instructional program needed substantial revision. The social studies program that existed during the early 1960s in the Mansfield City Schools was not designed to help meet the needs of boys and girls who were going to spend a great part of their lives in the twentieth and twenty-first centuries. The program was not articulated. Students were not being taught the necessary skills to find information and then make decisions based on known information. What was being learned had little meaning for what was happening in their everyday lives. There was no social studies curriculum in grades K-3. In grades 4, 5 and 6 the program was rigid, textbook-centered, and boring. It was also dominated by a single textbook approach, with the teacher doing most of the talking and dominating all of the other limited activities.

Individual teachers who were concerned about trying to improve the program were unaware of what was going on in terms of social studies teaching in the other grade levels throughout the school district. There was a tremendous void in communication among teachers with respect to what was happening in their individual classrooms. After enough individual teachers started to think about our program and what was happening in terms of change in other school districts relative to social studies, signs of excitement about the fact that something might be done to improve our social studies program began to appear.

One of the first activities involved a number of our social studies teachers at Mansfield Senior High School who wanted to break the lockstep pattern which tended to dominate the high school social studies program. In the 1961–62 school year a number of teachers met with the building principal and the assistant superintendent in charge of curriculum and expressed their frustration, concerns, and problems relative to our social studies program. The teachers also informed the principal and assistant superintendent that they had some ideas about how they could make a small beginning in developing a program which might better utilize the existing social studies materials and the strengths and weaknesses of the staff collectively in the Social Studies Department at Mansfield Senior High School. Several meetings were held. As thinking started to crystallize, it was decided that an effort should be made to have a type of team-teaching project in American history for the coming school year. Therefore, plans were laid so that during a certain period of the school day a number of teachers would plan together, work together, and try to come up with a viable, stimulating program which might open up new areas of interest for the students. This program was developed and implemented.

At the conclusion of the team-teaching project in American History, the staff evaluated the project. It also gathered some evaluation from the participating students. The data revealed both pro and con positions on this approach from teachers and students.

The pro points of view were:

1. Most teachers liked this because each teacher could utilize his/her knowledge and expertise in a given subject matter area.
2. The teacher in charge of the session only presented his/her lecture once, not four or five times in one day.
3. The other members of the teaching team could learn from the teacher in charge of the large group session.
4. The students liked this approach because they had an opportunity to experience several teaching styles in action, not just one.
5. The students' base of knowledge was greater from the team approach than from one individual teacher.
6. There was cooperative planning among the teachers.

The con points of view were:

1. There was some risk involved for each teacher because he/she was teaching in front of his/her peers. Some teachers did a better job of teaching than others. This made some teachers feel good and embarrassed others.
2. The students observed rather quickly that some teachers were better than others. This made some students feel uncomfortable, while others were proud to say "he/she is my teacher."

3. The approach required teachers to give up some individual identity. This bothered some teachers because in planning there were times when the majority ruled.
4. It was difficult to find an acceptable method on which a majority of teachers and students could agree concerning faculty testing of information presented in the large group sessions.
5. Some teachers felt the pressures of having to become selective on information to be presented in large group sessions.

After analyzing our experiences we felt we had gained several insights which would be very helpful in future efforts to change curriculum. Some of these insights included:

• Direct teacher involvement in change is a key element.
• Curriculum change is linked closely to positive attitudes of teachers and administrators.
• Curriculum change, as we had anticipated, is a long, tedious process.
• Time, outside the regular school year, is needed for developmental work. This arrangement removes the teachers from the everyday pressures of the classroom, so full concentration can be given to the task at hand.

During the same time period, when the high school project was being implemented, a number of individual teachers in the junior high and elementary schools had been working on new approaches and new materials in the teaching of social studies. Individual teachers recognized that they could only make limited progress in terms of district-wide improvement; therefore, a number of discussions were held involving elementary, junior high, and high school teachers to explore what could be done to improve our social studies curriculum district-wide. At about the same time, the Ford Foundation was making available to school districts across the United States fellowships in the humanities for individual teachers. These fellowships were designed to bring together interested teachers who had been screened, selected, and assigned to various college sites throughout the United States for summer sessions in the study of humanities. The programs helped to recharge the intellectual batteries of individual teachers, as well as to give teachers the opportunities to come together, brainstorm, discuss, and think about new ways of teaching and motivating students. The Mansfield City Schools were very fortunate to have their superintendent of schools and two of their high school classroom teachers chosen to participate in the John Hay Fellowship Program. The knowledge gained by the three individuals was to be very useful later on when the district made efforts to secure outside funds to help in the effort to improve social studies. The John Hay Fellowship also helped the individuals involved to develop into better educators in our school district.

At this time, we were well aware that funds were needed to pay teachers to come in after school and during the summer months to develop curriculum and instructional activities and to buy current instructional materials. Huge quantities of materials were needed if a K-12 effort were going to be made. There would also be a need for outside consultants who would bring their expertise. The district, however, did not have necessary funds to do the job.

One of the most important elements in any effort to improve an instructional program is the commitment to that program by the Board of Education. Prior to the submission of a proposal for federal funds to aid this project, the necessary groundwork had been laid with the Board of Education by holding workshop sessions for Board members in order to inform them of the desires and needs of the boys and girls in Mansfield. After several work sessions, members of the Board of Education encouraged the efforts to improve the social studies curriculum. When the time came to submit our application, the Board gave us 100% support. At that time, the Board also made the commitment that whatever curriculum developed during the three years of the grant would be continued as the basic social studies curriculum K-12 throughout the Mansfield City School District. In conjunction with the Board support, the Superintendent of Schools and the Director of Curriculum also gave high priority to the development and implementation of the social studies curriculum. The resources of the curriculum materials budget and the audio-visual and library budgets were concentrated on providing materials for the project to be carried forward and completed. The Supervisor of Library and Instructional Material Centers has been very cooperative throughout the entire effort to improve our social studies program. Each year she has purchased instructional materials which meet the needs of our social studies curriculum.

PHASE II: 1965–1967

The Elementary and Secondary Education Act was passed in 1965. This Act made available to qualifying districts funds which could be used to develop innovative and exemplary plans to improve education. A team of several teachers and administrators pursued the idea of writing an application to get funds to help with the development of the program. Late in the winter of 1966, the team worked for several weeks to write a proposal for funds for the development of a social studies curriculum, K-12.

The application tried to suggest innovations that might lead to a viable, dynamic K-12 social studies curriculum. A first step was to create a committee to develop social studies objectives. This committee included a broad representation of various segments of the Mansfield Community: i.e., labor, industrial, racial, ethnic, professional, civic, cultural, and commercial. Working with the committee were members of the Mansfield Board of Education, the teaching and administrative staff, and outside curriculum specialists and consultants.

Objectives

Examples of the objectives were:
1. To change a negative attitude toward social studies held by many students to a positive attitude toward social studies.
2. To develop learning experiences which would help bring about the desirable changes in student attitudes.
3. To determine the scope and sequence of the social studies curriculum.
4. To develop a K-12 social studies curriculum.
5. To set up a process to evaluate the effectiveness of the social studies curriculum.

The objectives then provided a sense of direction and were used to select content, methods, materials, and evaluation procedures. The scope and sequence pattern emerged from the objectives, and it became increasingly clear what the emphasis might be at each grade level. Another crucial part of the plan to bring about change and to develop a new social studies curriculum for the school district, begun in the summer of 1967, involved in-service education for the teachers and administrators. It included 18 K-12 teachers who had submitted letters of application to a screening committee which consisted of the directors of personnel, curriculum, elementary education, secondary education, and director of the project. The teachers formed the nucleus of the staff for the inservice program throughout the 1967–68 school year.

Many of the instructional materials were limited, inadequate, unrealistic, and too unsophisticated for a large number of our students. In addition, a substantial number of teachers were limiting themselves to one textbook. Students were asked to master and recall facts without exercising their rational power, and discussion was kept to a minimum. The changed plan called for the development of a multimedia approach. Materials included films, periodicals, filmstrips, books written at various levels, maps, tapes, recordings, manuscripts, original documents, facsimiles, pictures, charts, etc. The materials were to be housed and available in instructional materials centers. Materials were gathered from distributors of various instructional media, other school systems, community agencies, and the many curriculum development centers at universities. Previously some materials were acquired from such sources as Asian Studies, Joint Council on Economic Education, Educational Services, Inc., the Curriculum Center at Pennsylvania, the Center at San Francisco State College, the Sociological Resources for Secondary Schools at the University of Michigan, the Center on History, Amherst College, the Center at Syracuse University, and the Harvard University Project. Additional materials were gathered from other programs as they were developed. Examples of programs were those of the University of Illinois, the University of Georgia, and the University of Minnesota. Materials that were in accord with the district objectives and approaches were incorporated into the Mansfield Program. The next big source of materials for the teacher inservice program was from the local area: the public library, families, area parochial schools, industry, individuals, community agencies, the Richland County Historical Society, and the Richland County Chapter of the Ohio Genealogical Society. As teachers worked with various resources, they developed kits which became part of the classroom and the social studies materials centers for use by students and teachers.

Many teachers felt that the basic approach to the teaching of social studies in the past had been too expository. Students were told everything in a stereotypic lecture. An important goal—the development of insights and understandings, the ability to think—was not achieved. Therefore, teachers planned to seek ways to implement new teaching concepts and approaches with more emphasis on inquiry, inductive thinking, reflection, and independent study.

A local diary (an American Civil War diary given to the schools for reproduction by the family of William Mosey) exemplifies the use of primary material, raw data, to inspire inquiry into what the Civil War was really like. In addition, teachers used diaries kept by young boys in the Confederate Army, World War II, and the Vietnam War. Students were encouraged to compare the diaries and discover the similarities and dissimilarities of different wars and different periods of history and of the individual writers.

Many subjects and teachers were compartmentalized in approaching social studies courses. Compartmentalization tended to isolate the history course from other disciplines. Teachers tended to limit themselves to certain pet areas or just their strong points; consequently, many important areas of American history courses were not studied or were only given cursory attention. Individual weaknesses could be attacked by creating a team of American history teachers who would work, plan, and teach together. This approach would permit more flexibility in selecting the areas of history to be emphasized. The three decades (1830–1860) of the Ante-Bellum Period serve as an illustration. A team of teachers was organized to expand the eighth-grade American history into an eighth-grade American Civilization Program on the 1830s to the 1860s. The team would be expanded by including teachers who represented other disciplines, such as art, literature, music, drama, journalism, economics, sociology, and political science. Qualified community persons, such as an architect and a university professor of education, would add other dimensions to the three decades of 1830 to 1860 in American civilization. This approach would utilize the various disciplines and enlist the full resources of the school and community, as well as the full talents of teachers.

PHASE III: 1967–1968

In the winter of 1967, we had already laid the groundwork in terms of arranging for consultants to work with us on our social studies project if our application for a grant were approved. For example, at that time, we had contacted Melvin Arnoff, Assistant Professor of Elementary Education at Kent State University; Harris L. Dante, Professor of History and Social Studies Education at Kent State University; L. Warren Nelson, Professor of Social Studies Education at Miami, Ohio; Raymond H. Muessig, Professor of Social Studies Education at The Ohio State University; M. Eugene Gilliom, Professor of Social Studies Education at The Ohio State University; and I. Keith Tyler, Professor of Education at The Ohio State University. Two social studies consultants from the State Department of Education, Charles Loparo and Byron H. Walker, also were contacted and had agreed to consult with us on the project. We felt that people of this caliber and knowledge would be very valuable to us as we developed and implemented the ideas which we had formulated.

The workshop during the summer of 1967 brought together consultants and teachers, K-12, with varied ranges of teaching experience, to begin the task that lay ahead of them. The attitude toward change and building a new curriculum was good. The workshop proved to be fruitful in the sense that teachers were together discussing new ideas, concepts, programs, and ways of stimulating and motivating students. The consultants brought from their various perspectives ideas of what was happening relative to the social studies field. Each consultant in his or her own unique way was able to contribute immensely to the overall environment and knowledge of the workshop. The teachers began to develop materials and interact among themselves. Overall, it was a productive summer. For the first time, many of the teachers in the workshop had been exposed not only to new ideas and high-powered consultants but also to new materials which were coming on the market. The opportunities afforded in the workshop gave our teachers ample opportunity to examine and scrutinize many materials, some of which were ultimately selected to be used in our classrooms in the ensuing school year.

At the close of the workshop, the 18 participating teachers were asked to complete an evaluation form expressing their judgments on the overall success of the workshop. The items which they felt most helpful concerning the workshop were as follows:

1. an opportunity to conduct experimental classes and to observe other instructors conducting classes.
2. demonstrations by consultants in actual class situations.

3. experiencing use of new methods and materials and access to them, such as transparencies, color lift process, films, filmstrips, records, and tapes.
4. buzz sessions with other participants and consultants involving challenging ideas and philosophies.
5. classroom experience with different kinds of children.
6. opportunities to actually develop or produce new and different teaching methods.
7. freedom of teacher participants to experiment without fear of failure or embarrassment.
8. assistance by consultants in drawing up goals, objectives, concepts, and generalizations for teaching units.
9. good rapport among participants.
10. a workshop that was just about the right length.

Seven weeks gave an ample amount of time to do the job. Each participating teacher found the workshop to be useful in some respect.

During the 1967–68 school year 18 teachers left the summer workshop enthusiastic about the new materials and ideas which they were going to be using in their classrooms. Teachers were able to draw on consultant help during the school year. Teachers were given opportunities to visit each others' classes to observe and to make suggestions. Also teachers were given released time for full days to demonstrate their best lessons for each other to stimulate and inspire each other. Some teachers taught other teachers' classes.

The knowledge that there would be continuous administrative assistance and support, as well as long-term, readily available help from consultants, bolstered the teachers' enthusiasm as they went about the school year. Some of the materials and ideas involved: Families Around the World in grade one; Economic Understandings, economics unit in grade four; Understanding Others in grade four; and looking at public issues in grades nine through twelve. New materials and new books, such as *Johnny Tremain*, were purchased and used to give more in-depth study of the Revolutionary War. Many teachers had an opportunity to go to other school districts for firsthand observation of some of the new and exciting things that were happening in classrooms. The following are some examples of the experiences and conferences in which Mansfield teachers participated:

- five secondary teachers went to Lakewood High School, Ohio, to observe and discuss their world history and American history program.
- four secondary teachers and a high school principal journeyed to Parma High School, Ohio, to gather and adapt ideas from the humanities program there.
- the project director and a teacher traveled to several curriculum centers in the Chicago area. Among those were the NCA Foreign Relations Project, the Industrial Relations Center, and the Anthropology Curriculum Study Project.
- four secondary teachers toured the Social Studies Curriculum Center at Carnegie-Mellon University and observed classes in two Pittsburgh high schools where new approaches to social studies were being tested.
- seven elementary teachers drove to an elementary school in Berea, Ohio, to observe the Greater Cleveland Council of Social Studies program in operation.
- two teachers went to schools in the Boston area and the Lincoln Filene Center for Citizenship and Public Affairs at Tufts University in regard to the units developed there on cultural diversity.
- four secondary teachers, a high school principal, and a junior high principal attended a Title III NDEA Conference in Columbus, Ohio. Edwin Fenton and John Gibson were the key speakers.
- two teachers attended a workshop at a high school in Columbus where John Good, formerly with Edwin Fenton at Carnegie-Mellon, headed a program on inquiry teaching.

These excursions gave participating teachers insights into the process of curriculum building which they could not have obtained through conventional means.

The 1967–68 inservice education program for teachers included prominent persons from the social studies field. These resource people came to the district and talked with staff on the trends and innovations of the day. Charles Keller, Professor of History at Williams College and Director of the John Hay Fellows Program in the Humanities, spoke at the first general inservice meeting on Wednesday, October 4, 1967. Training sessions were provided for teachers to practice and discuss concepts that were going to be employed. These sessions met one day a week after school for ten to twelve weeks during each semester.

A significant dimension of the program was the high interest level displayed by various community groups in what was being done to build a new social studies curriculum. Groups included the Mayor's Committee on Human Relations, the American Association of University Women, the League of Women Voters, the Parent-Teacher Association Council, the Richland County Genealogical Society, and the Richland County Historical Society.

The historical and genealogical societies helped curriculum workers gather local resource materials that could be used to enrich the social studies curriculum at various levels. These materials concentrated on the history of Mansfield and its relationship to the various social studies concepts with which we were working in such areas as:

- the power structure of early Mansfield.
- the economic development of Mansfield.
- religions and church history.
- famous local personalities, including women and members of various ethnic and racial groups.
- the various professions.
- Mansfield music and other fine arts.
- architectural design trends.
- ethnic and population analysis.
- recreation in the nineteenth century.

During the 1967–68 school year, we found that most of the teachers were agreeable to and enthusiastic about using new teaching concepts and approaches. These approaches were being supplemented by more direct student involvement in classroom work. Perhaps the greatest change was the effect the new program had upon the teachers. Many teachers had gotten away from strictly textbook teaching; they were using many supplemental materials. More teachers realized how important it was to assist students in developing understandings (concepts and generalizations), skills, and attitudes. There was a spirit of experimentation among teachers. Many teachers were eager to try new materials and methods. Whenever a teacher expressed an idea to try something, that teacher was encouraged to pursue his/her experiment.

One other interesting observation came from A. T. Dickinson,

Jr., the administrator for the Mansfield Public Library. He observed an increased use of library resources. Several teachers had, in fact, worked with him on various projects. He was impressed with the creative imagination many teachers were showing, and added that he would be hard pressed to keep up with the teachers if this kind of approach continued to expand. He also indicated that the library would be very cooperative and helpful in trying to make more teachers aware of the valuable resources a local library can provide to such a curriculum project.

PHASE IV: 1968–1969

In the spring of 1968, the Mansfield City Schools prepared and submitted a proposal for a continuation grant so the accomplishments of the 1967–68 school year could be continued. The application was approved, and Mansfield was awarded a second year grant of $75,923.00.

The objectives in the original proposal would be continued. Those objectives were:

1. to reconstruct the social studies education curriculum so that it would be congruent with the reality of twentieth-century living.
2. to redefine our social studies objectives.
3. to establish inservice education.
4. to structure a scope and sequence.
5. to use multimedia material.
6. to implement new teaching concepts and approaches.

The second-year grant facilitated continued efforts to achieve these objectives. In the grant we would be working on two additional objectives: development and implementation of resource units, and inservice education. The resource unit required the use of new teaching methods and materials; consequently, inservice training would be required.

Successful implementation and acceptance by teachers, K-12, of the new curriculum was a vital part of the project. In view of this, it was essential that a teacher with elementary training and teaching experience be added to the project staff. The project would then be implemented by one elementary social studies resource teacher, one secondary social studies resource teacher, and the project director, who would be working full time throughout the 1968–69 school year. It was imperative that the project have two full-time resource teachers available to help teachers develop new ideas and new approaches, as well as maintain that which had already been developed.

At the conclusion of the unit writing workshop in August, 1968, the participants were asked to evaluate the workshop and to offer suggestions for possible improvement of future unit writing workshops. Overall, the participants considered the preliminary work done in the workshop to be both essential and beneficial. The most highly valued aspect of this segment of the workshop was the opportunity to examine a wide variety of materials, including texts and audio-visual materials. Some participants selected materials to be incorporated into the units. Small group meetings, meetings with the consultants, and determination of objectives were beneficial results of preliminary work. Frustration was experienced by the teachers as they tried to write their thoughts and convey them to other teachers. Some teachers could not agree upon which grade level certain units should be assigned. Agreement was reached following the year's use of the units in the classroom. Another helpful feature of the workshop was considered to be the availability of research materials, including professional social studies texts, an extensive file of publishers' catalogs, and units written by teachers for use in other communities. Most of the participants found the atmosphere of the workshop conducive to the actual writing of units, especially the discipline of scheduled hours for writing, freedom from classroom responsibilities, and discussion with other unit writers. Unrestricted space, adequate supplies, and the indispensable work of the two typists were highly valued. The majority of the participants considered the time spent with consultants to be of major importance. There was general agreement on the need for more time available with consultants, both on an individual basis and in group meetings.

By the beginning of the 1968–69 school year, 12 units were ready to be piloted throughout the school district in various classrooms. These units were:

Kindergarten—New Horizons
First Grade—Urban Families
Second Grade—Food for Mansfield
Third Grade—Farm Community
Fourth Grade—Map Skills
Fifth Grade—Colonial America

Sixth Grade—The Andean Region
Seventh Grade—Industries
Eighth Grade—Independence and Freedom
Tenth Grade—Cultural Evolution of Man
Eleventh Grade—Immigration
American Foreign Policy

Several thousand dollars were spent on materials and equipment necessary for the teachers to implement properly the various units written and developed during the summer workshop of 1968. Whenever possible, identical units were placed in schools in which the background and the ability levels of the students differed. After the units were pilot tested, teachers had an opportunity to teach the materials and to evaluate content. They suggested changes which would be examined and reviewed for the revision before city-wide adoption.

Throughout the 1968–69 school year, considerable progress was made by those teachers who piloted the units. Actual changes could be observed in the attitudes of many teachers. As each teacher completed his or her unit, the project staff evaluated his/her experiences. These experiences became the basis for the unit which would be implemented city-wide the coming school year.

The teachers who had actually written the units, with the help of the consultants, were the ones who demonstrated the greatest change in their attitude toward teaching techniques. The unit writers were also the ones who became the backbone of the teaching corps working with the units. The best way to have teachers implement new materials was to involve the teachers in the development of those materials. In the process of being involved, teachers developed a commitment to the program and became the best salespersons of the program to the other teachers in the district. The opportunity to have a consultant nearby, as the units were developed, was also a vital ingredient. Unit writing is a highly sophisticated, and yet frustrating, experience. Therefore, as the unit is developed, it is necessary to have a professional consultant available who can read the material, react, and help the teacher through the overall process.

The Title III ESEA Project to develop a K-12 social studies curriculum had a substantial impact on many of the teachers in Mansfield. The summer workshops scheduled in this project clearly demonstrated that constructive and creative curriculum work can best be accomplished during the summer. It also is important that the local school district be willing to contribute to the development, as well as to utilize outside funds from a project. The enthusiasm shown by teachers and students trying new things in social studies created interest for change in other instructional departments in the school district. An important factor in this was the publicity that was given to the social studies project, and to the students and teachers involved in the project. The social studies project had done much to show the community that the school system was trying to improve the curriculum to better meet the needs of boys and girls.

PHASE V: 1969–1970

During the spring of 1969, the application for a continuation grant of the original project was submitted. Mansfield's request for a budget of $50,063.00 for the 1969–70 school year was approved. This money was used to continue the inservice education for the teachers, to buy materials, and to pay unit writers and consultants to develop new units and revise the pilot units.

During the summer of 1969, another workshop was held for our social studies staff. In addition to involving teachers who had previous experiences in writing units, new teachers were invited into the program each summer. This corps of teachers would serve as the backbone of the social studies curriculum K-12. Unit writers were selected, and consultants were engaged for the summer activity. Again the summer workshop was stimulating and rewarding. Teachers were able to move very quickly through the process, yet do good work. The availability of many materials, in an area where teachers could work along with consultants, was conducive to an overall successful summer workshop. During the workshop, a number of units were revised, and new units were written. By the beginning of the 1969–70 school year, 19 social studies units K-12 which would be taught systemwide were complete. The units were:

Kindergarten—New Horizons
First Grade—Urban Families
Second Grade—Food for Mansfield
Third Grade—Farm Communities
Fourth Grade—Map Skills
India
Understanding Others

Fifth Grade—Colonial America
A Journey Through East Africa
Sixth Grade—The Andean Region
Seventh Grade—Early Ohio
Industries in Ohio
Education in Ohio
Eighth Grade—Independence and Freedom
Westward Expansion
Tenth Grade—Cultural Evolution of Man
Man and the Development of Ideologies
Eleventh Grade—Immigration
American Foreign Policy

In addition to the 19 units ready to be taught system-wide, 20 other units were in the process of being developed so that they would be piloted in selected schools throughout the school district. These units were:

Kindergarten—Fun and Beauty Around the World
First Grade—Families in Japan
My Family
Second Grade—Government Services
Families in Russia
Third Grade—A European Community
Fifth Grade—An Overview of the U.S.A.
Regional Study of the Midwest
Washington, D.C.
New York City
Sixth Grade—An Overview of South America
A Study of Manaus
A Study of São Paulo
Seventh Grade—Government of Ohio
Geography of Ohio
Tenth Grade—Man and the Development of Nationalism
and Internationalism
Man and the Development of Science and
Technology
Man and His Search for Meaning in Life
and in a Changing World
Eleventh Grade—Politics and Government
The Economic Development of America

Throughout the 1969–70 school year, efforts were continued in teaching, piloting, and revising units. One technique which the resource teachers used was that of sharing with other staff members any unique ideas or activities which they observed teachers using in the classrooms. As the resource teachers would identify new experiences in the classrooms, they were written up and sent to all other teachers who were teaching that same unit. This process was not only a good, quick way to continue revision, but it also gave particular teachers some measure of public recognition for their work.

By this time, the requests from other districts to observe Mansfield's classrooms or obtain materials that had been developed were becoming numerous. In fact, during the 1969–70 school year, over 100 requests from districts throughout the United States were processed.

Consultants came in periodically and observed teachers teaching the resource social studies units. This technique was effective; it offered the consultants opportunities to see firsthand actual classroom operation of units which the consultants had helped the teachers develop during the previous summer. It also gave consultants opportunities to make on-the-spot analyses and then suggest revision and/or inservice work. As the third year of the project money ended, we felt a sound K-12 social studies curriculum had been developed.

After the project funding ended, the Board of Education paid, out of local monies, a social studies supervisor and two resource teachers to provide overall supervision and direction for the newly developed social studies curriculum. Local monies were also budgeted to develop other resource units, plan an inservice education summer program, purchase materials, and pay consultants. During the 1970 summer workshop, new units were produced and units which had previously been tested and piloted were revised and updated. Examples of these units were:

Second Grade—Clothing
                Housing
    Third Grade—The Paris Community
    Fourth Grade—Economics
    Sixth Grade—Brazil
                Egypt
  Seventh Grade—Economics and Industry
  Eighth Grade—The Constitution and Formation of U.S.
                Government
                American Civil War

Eleventh Grade—Problems in Municipal Government
Civil War, Reconstruction and Negro in America
American Culture in the Twentieth Century

By the end of the 1970 summer unit writing workshop, more than 100 teachers in the school district had been directly involved in the development of the curriculum; these teachers became the foundation of the curriculum.

At the conclusion of the social studies project, there was an opportunity to apply for a project in the Ohio career education movement. Fortunately, Mansfield was one of those districts chosen to be a pilot participant. This meant that the district would be the recipient of money to develop a career education program for Mansfield's schools. The social studies curriculum became the vehicle whereby career education would be incorporated into the elementary classrooms. A spin-off was that career education provided opportunities to purchase materials which not only met the needs of career education, but also helped meet the needs of the ongoing social studies curriculum. The interrelation among various instructional programs is a "must" if a project of any magnitude is expected to be successful.

It has now been seven school years since the social studies project funding ended. During that period, resources had been managed to the point where some degree of success of the program had been maintained, including revision and updating of the curriculum.

PHASE VI: 1971–1977

The Mansfield District, as with many other systems, has experienced financial difficulties. During the 1974–75 school year, reduced funds resulted in the elimination of a number of faculty positions. Unfortunately, the two social studies resource teacher positions, among others, were dropped. In August, 1971, the Social Studies Supervisor became the Director of Personnel. It was agreed, however, that as Director of Personnel, the duties of the Social Studies Supervisor would be carried out and maintained as fully as possible to continue those efforts made. At the beginning of the 1975–76 school year, there was not adequate help to maintain the social studies curriculum as desired. Consequently, a number of the plans which had been laid have been rather slow in implementation. However, in spite of the adverse circumstances, some progress has been made in the social studies curriculum.

In the 1975–76 school year, a committee consisting of a representative of each of the twenty schools, along with several administrators, was created. This committee became known as the Social Studies Curriculum Review Committee. The committee was charged with the basic responsibility of developing an evaluation instrument which would be used to survey the teaching staff to determine what direction the social studies curriculum should take in the future. The committee was very active through the 1975–76 and 1976–77 school years, working with its overall charge.

The survey taken in 1975–76 by the committee indicated that the overwhelming majority of the teachers who teach the social studies units were in favor of maintaining the basic thrust of the social studies program which had been developed earlier under the three-year project. This meant that the objectives, scope and sequence, and the resource unit approach would be maintained as central features of the curriculum. The committee recognized, however, that a number of units were in need of revision and updating. New materials would have to be purchased to maintain the program.

One unique outcome of the curriculum work in 1975–76 was the creation of a class for Mansfield teachers on the Mansfield Ohio State University Campus during the spring of 1976. This class had 18 enrollees, all of whom, except for two, were teachers in the Mansfield City School District. Not only did this course carry college credit, it afforded the unique opportunity for teachers to get together in a type of inservice training and develop new units as well as revise existing units. A number of units were developed during the course. The course was followed up in the summer of 1976 with another unit-writing workshop involving two teachers. The work which had been started in the course was continued in the workshop. The units that were developed are now used in the classrooms. Examples of new units developed were:

Second Grade—Map Skills
Third Grade—Using a Globe
Fifth Grade—American Folk Heroes
Sixth Grade—Decision Making

Sub-committees of the Social Studies Curriculum Review Committee have identified materials to go along with those units which were designated as the ones to be updated and revised. This workshop began in the spring of 1977, involving ten teachers to revise existing units and create new ones. The units revised were:

> First Grade—American Family
> Japanese Family
> Second Grade—Clothing
> Third Grade—Mexican Community
> Fifth Grade—Exploration
> Sixth Grade—Middle East
> Seventh Grade—Applied Geography Skills
> Ninth Grade—Consumer Economics
> Tenth Grade—Cultural Evolution of Man
> Ideologies
> Eleventh Grade—American Culture in the Twentieth Century

An example of a new unit developed was:

> Kindergarten—The Farm

Still another unique opportunity for our social studies efforts occurred in the spring of 1976. The school district received a grant to participate in the Institute on Political and Legal Education (IPLE) Project out of New Jersey. For a full week in May of 1976 the project staff from the IPLE Center came to Mansfield and conducted a week-long workshop for all of our high school social studies teachers. This workshop prepared the teachers for work during the summer of 1976 in the writing and preparation of IPLE government materials. These units were taught on a pilot basis in classrooms in the two high schools throughout the 1976–77 school year. Much of the IPLE Program will eventually be in the units on government.

During the 1977–78 school year, the units developed and revised during the summer of 1977 are being taught in the schools, while existing units are being reviewed for future revisions. The plans are to continue unit revisions and curriculum development in another workshop in the summer of 1978.

As of now, the Mansfield City School District social studies curriculum K-12 includes 58 units which are articulated and correlated sequentially. It is a curriculum that is better than the program that existed ten years ago; yet it has the potential of becoming even more meaningful for the boys and girls, as long as teachers, administrators, the Board of Education, and the community are committed to this end.

Insights Gained from Mansfield's Experiences

As a result of their endeavors, the Mansfield City Schools have reached the following tentative conclusions, which may be useful to curriculum reformers elsewhere in the nation:

1. The processes learned and perfected in sound, perennial social studies curriculum work can be readily transferred to program development in other fields, such as English and career education, thereby conserving funds and avoiding previous mistakes. Enthusiasm can be contagious, too, and inspired social studies teachers may ignite their colleagues in science and mathematics.

2. The social studies curriculum provides one of the best mechanisms for integrating learning in other subject areas. Teachers in social studies, English, science, mathematics, art, music, speech, industrial technology, career education, etc. can work cooperatively to help students approach broad, important understandings in an organized fashion.

3. Each social studies resource unit developed for use throughout the school district should contain more alternative ideas than any one teacher could possibly use. There should be certain key resource units taught by every teacher at each grade level so basic learnings can be developed on a district-wide basis in an additive, expansive manner. And there should be more optional units at all grade levels than any single teacher could utilize, so teachers can accommodate the very special needs and interests of their individual classes.

4. A school district that is really serious about improving its social studies curriculum should maintain a continuous, long-term relationship with one outside K-12 social studies consultant or with an elementary person and a secondary specialist who work closely with each other. It takes time for an outsider to become familiar with the unique needs, interests, problems, and goals of a school district, to find the best ways of helping and working with teachers and others, and to earn the respect and affection of curriculum workers. From time to time, as special situations arise and desires are identified, numerous other con-

sultants can be brought in for as long as they are required; but continuity is best served by one or two outside people who care about a district's progress over the years.

5. Involving individuals, groups, businesses, industries, libraries, museums, colleges, universities, etc. not only improves the social studies curriculum, but also enhances public relations.

6. When resource teachers are needed and can be afforded to help classroom teachers implement new curriculum improvements, it is better to select these resource teachers from the most experienced, capable, creative, respected, liked, and energetic people in the existing faculty than to search for outsiders. Resource teachers are often the first to observe classroom teachers and the most likely to be in classrooms frequently. They must get along well initially and wear well over an extended period of time. They need to know the city and its public, schools, and children well and to be aware of where help is most needed and desired. They are the easiest persons to absorb back into classrooms if there are budgetary cuts or if their services become less necessary for a time. When resource teachers do return to local district classrooms, they become even more credible to their fellow teachers.

7. With the current, meager level of financial support for social studies curriculum improvement in most school districts all over the United States, it is better to do a *good* job of revising and updating a few existing resource units and of creating a small number of new resource units each year—on an individual basis, as required and wanted—than it is to let everything slide for four or five years and then to do a *poor* job of working on an entire program. Limited funds can sometimes be secured to give 1-4 teachers released time or one- or two-week summer employment for curriculum work, where the sums to support numerous teachers are now unavailable.

8. It is better to have several teachers—who are teaching the same social studies units—share larger, more complete and varied, traveling multimedia kits than it is to attempt to provide each teacher with fewer, duplicative instructional materials.

9. Providing social studies teachers with opportunities to go to other schools, districts, project centers, and professional conferences not only gives curriculum workers insights into processes of program improvement which they could not obtain through more conventional means, but it also gives them a wel-

come, needed break from their daily routines. Morale is extremely important in long-range curricular undertakings.

10. Outside social studies project money is used best when a school district has a long-term commitment to continuous social studies curriculum improvement. Reforms which last only for the duration of funding may serve some purposes, but important, enduring social studies goals are much more likely to be achieved when there is a solid foundation on which to build enriched learnings made possible by additional financial resources.

11. It is better to seek outside funding to support social studies curriculum improvements genuinely needed and desired by local classroom teachers than it is to find out first what various agencies, foundations, projects, etc. will finance and then to try to persuade teachers to implement those types of alterations.

12. Resource teachers, principals, supervisors, central office administrators, outside consultants, representatives of funding agencies, parents, and others can help and inspire social studies teachers greatly by investing substantial blocks of time in classrooms—observing, participating in learning activities, serving as sources of enabling and enriching ideas, teaching, demonstrating fresh approaches, and the like. Classroom teachers' performance and morale can be advanced greatly when they know that others share their concerns with respect to providing all children and youth with the best possible education.

3
Curriculum Improvement: A Sampler of Noteworthy Experiences

Jo Ann Cutler Sweeney and Gloria Contreras

Introduction

Change in human behavior is not easy. Curriculum change, which involves deeply held beliefs about the kind of citizens we want for the future, should not be undertaken lightly. The "curriculum" refers to courses offered by educational institutions or in a particular subject field within a school setting. Many schools consider not only the courses offered, but the total school program as part of the curriculum.

Expanding knowledge of child development and changing needs of society demand continuing consideration of school curricula. Change is not automatically the needed response. Thoughtful review can highlight existing program strengths which should be continued. This chapter provides useful information about how some schools have dealt with curriculum review. Sometimes, with the best of motives, we tackle problems head-on without learning about the experience of others and the antecedents of so-called "new" programs and ideas. One of our strengths as a nation has been the willingness to face the frontier

JO ANN CUTLER SWEENEY is Associate Professor of Social Studies Education, College of Education, The University of Texas at Austin, Texas. GLORIA CONTRERAS is Assistant Professor of Social Studies Education, College of Education, The University of Texas at Austin, Texas.

and its unknowns. Nevertheless, in the case of curriculum reform, a historical perspective and sharing of knowledge may make the journey less arduous.

Flexibility and a sense of humor about ourselves are absolutely necessary for successful curriculum review. Working together invariably involves compromise and a willingness to listen to others. The development of school curriculum in a democracy is not restricted to the experts. Rather, input from a wide variety of interested persons is essential for effective program development.

Resistance to even creative change is frequently encountered. All of us can probably identify with a "theme of resistance to change." The cast of players may be different in your personal experience, but the basic plot is the same. You may have encountered: The administrator who responds, "We don't have the equipment," or "The community won't like it." The experienced teacher who reminds everyone, "We tried that in 1934, and it didn't work." The regionalist who informs everyone, "Good idea, but that won't work in this section of the country." The practical contributor who suggests, "It is true that the textbook is racist and sexist, but we have 75,000 copies." The solid defender of the *status quo* who tells the group, "Don't forget, we have always done it this way." Or maybe the "realist" who says, "We don't have enough help and we don't have the time." In spite of such resistance, creative curriculum change is possible. Keeping a sense of perspective helps.

The curriculum projects reviewed in this chapter are divided into three categories: (1) curriculum changes in social studies programs, (2) cross-disciplinary change projects, and (3) generic curriculum change prototypes.

The literature of curriculum improvement provided many possible examples for this chapter. Curriculum change is being generated throughout the country at all levels of instruction and across disciplines. Only a sampling is represented in this chapter. A variety of models is included. Salient points from each of the examples discussed should be helpful to schools contemplating curriculum review. Examples are not discussed in equal detail. Some, such as the West Islip Social Studies Program, are reported in more detail; while others, such as the Twin Cities Social Studies Service Center and the DEEP project, are described more briefly.

Curriculum Change and the Social Studies—
Right in Our Own Back Yard

This section provides information on curriculum change within the social studies area. Examples include the West Islip Public Schools Program, the Social Studies Field Agent Training Program, the Twin Cities Social Studies Service Center, and the Development Economic Education Program.

West Islip Public Schools Project—Situation SOS

The West Islip project can be described as a case of "If we did it, you can do it, too!" Envision School District "SOS." It lacks district-wide goals and objectives for the elementary social studies. The curriculum is neither interdisciplinary nor sequential. District-wide coordination is poor. Evaluation is tantamount to the traditional testing of textbook content at a low cognitive level. Permanent funding for the social studies is nonexistent. What can School District SOS do to install a modern social studies program? Read on; there is a happy ending!

Situation SOS comes close to describing the elementary social studies program as it was in the New York West Islip School District. Program deficiencies were pinpointed by using curriculum guidelines developed by the National Council for Social Studies and the State of New York. Recognition of the weaknesses of the social studies program prompted the formation of a social studies steering committee made up of six West Islip classroom teachers and two school principals selected jointly by the superintendent of schools and the president of the West Islip Teachers Association. The steering committee undertook to answer three basic questions relevant to curriculum improvement: Where are we? Where do we want to be? How will we get there?

The first question, "Where are we?", was in all likelihood answered with "Not where we want to be." The question "Where do we want to be?" led to the development of a framework outlining their goals. First, it spelled out that there should be an emphasis on the teaching of social science concepts, rather than on the accumulation of low-level facts. Second, students needed to learn to cope with pressing social problems. Third, a sequential development of skills and research techniques was deemed important. Fourth, there was a need for exhibiting inquiry and discovery teaching techniques. Fifth, a more interdisciplinary approach should be used. Finally, they identified a need for the use of multimedia resources.

The question "How do we get there?" was resolved when the committee agreed to field test programs that satisfied the requirements of a modern social studies curriculum as previously outlined. Teacher volunteers were to be used to field test the programs.

Important to interject is the fact that, in the meantime, the West Islip Board of Education newsletter had publicized the impending curriculum improvement project. Dissatisfaction with the existing social studies curriculum increased as the faculty became better informed of the work of the steering committee through the distribution of additional timely literature. Faculty interest in social studies was further enhanced through skillful use of resource people, visitations to schools with recommended social studies programs, attendance at professional conferences, and presentations of new social studies materials by publishers. Doubtless the publicity the project received increased the interest of teachers in volunteering to field test new social studies programs.

During the field test period, a lack of communication between pilot teachers and steering committee members became apparent. To help resolve this problem, committee members or their representatives were assigned as "helpers" to provide general assistance and support for the teachers. The school district used a model of curriculum evaluation to measure progress toward their goals.

Project effectiveness was also measured by four evaluative instruments: the West Islip performance objectives, the *National Council for the Social Studies Guidelines Checklist*,[1] a survey based on the *Social Science Education Consortium Data Book*.[2] and the Remmers attitudinal scale measuring attitude toward any school subject.

More information about the installation of a modern social studies program in grades 4-6 in the West Islip Public Schools is available from the unpublished dissertation by Andrew A. Pecorro, Nova University, December 1975.[3]

What is the relationship between the West Islip experience and "principles" identified in the first chapter of this Bulletin? First, was the process of curriculum improvement more important than the product? Check. The steering committee, given almost insurmountable obstacles, proposed and implemented a program design and provided for the integration of the program into the district's permanent system. Participating teachers interacted with each other by sharing concerns about the program, as well as the sparse materials.

Chapter I suggests a second important point of curriculum development. The classroom teacher is the alpha and omega of curriculum improvement. Check. As noted, the steering committee was composed primarily of teachers who were seriously concerned about the quality of the social studies program in the West Islip School District. A third suggestion in Chapter I is that total dependence on teacher involvement can have some drawbacks. Participation in the field testing of programs at West Islip was on a voluntary basis. The steering committee was limited to a workable number of concerned individuals with the ability to make the entire curriculum improvement project a successful experience.

Fourth, curriculum change need not be followed by an entire district, grade level, or school. The original goal of the steering committee was to implement a modern social studies program at grade levels K-6. However, the project only involved grades 4-6 because of a lack of volunteers at grade levels K-3. Rather than force the program upon these grade levels, the project focused instead on grades 4-6. Finally, Chapter I warns that there are few "bargain prices" in curriculum improvement. Note that in the West Islip experience, the steering committee members responded to the problem of inadequate communication between themselves and the pilot teachers by assigning committee members as "helpers" to teachers in an effort to provide needed assistance and support. That is, the steering committee continued to play an active role throughout the curriculum improvement process.

What can we learn from the West Islip School District experience in curriculum improvement? As stated, if West Islip did it, so can you. The basic procedure for implementing change in West Islip furnishes a systematically sound model for use by other school districts or schools. First, conduct a needs assessment of the existing social studies program. Second, obtain both a goal and financial commitment to a social studies program from the Board of Education or administration. Third, obtain a commitment from the faculty to the goals and objectives of the program. Fourth, publicize the program that is underway to provide an awareness of impending changes, especially if the project is to expand to others in the district or school. Fifth, provide a vehicle for coordination and evaluation of the program.

Social Studies Field Agent Training Program— Select Strong People

The Social Studies Field Agent Training Program developed at Indiana University is another approach to curriculum change.[4] This program tested the feasibility of training social studies teachers who would then return to their local districts to disseminate information about social studies programs. Evaluation of program effectiveness showed that field agents should be chosen who already exercise a respected leadership position in the school district. This experience also showed that field agents needed inservice help and evaluation packages for implementation in their respective school districts. Results further indicated that a stable teacher population is a significant factor in curriculum change.

If your school is thinking about change, you can benefit from what they learned. District support for the curriculum effort should be secured. Careful thought should go into the selection process of the change agents: you *need* respected leaders. Preplanning needs to be done and inservice help is not a luxury but the meat on the bones. A stable teacher population is the bottom line for real change.

Twin Cities Social Studies Service Center— Cooperation Pays Off

The Twin Cities Social Service Center suggests that two heads may really be better than one.[5] A center was designed to help individual classroom teachers, offer inservice training, and provide professional staff from the center to work with schools on curriculum development. School districts pooled resources to provide this central facility for curriculum change.

The center developed a depository of nationally developed curriculum projects, supplementary materials, center-developed materials, publisher-developed current social studies materials, locally developed social studies curriculum guides, and classroom materials. In addition to accumulating materials, center staff also:

1. sponsored meetings, workshops, demonstrations, and courses at the center and other locations to inform teachers about curriculum materials, strategies of instruction, and curriculum implementation;
2. provided consultation for the development of inservice training programs; and
3. consulted with school districts on the analysis of social studies materials.

Because districts pooled resources, the Twin Cities Center was able to provide a more comprehensive resource for curriculum change.

Development Economic Education Program (DEEP)—Teachers Can't Do It All

A process of curriculum improvement has been developed by the Joint Council on Economic Education.[6] A curriculum committee is appointed to undertake an assessment of the district's needs. A search stage follows in which school personnel identify resources in their area related to economic education. These contacts include consultants and existing curriculum materials. Evaluation suggests this process was successful, but there were difficulties with quality control of teacher-designed materials. Teachers are not incapable of designing effective classroom materials; however, committees of teachers often do not have the time, money, and resources for extensive curriculum writing.

The DEEP program stresses the importance of teacher involvement, especially if the curriculum change is to have staying power; however, this doesn't mean teachers have to start from scratch. Existing materials may answer identified curriculum needs. Teachers working with experienced curriculum writers may provide a compromise. Professional leaves of absence and paid summers may be another way to involve teachers actively in developing curriculum materials.

Cross-disciplinary Curriculum Projects—Learning a Lot from These, Too

The programs described in this section include the Foxfire Project, the Mendocino College Interdisciplinary Education Project, the Adult Performance Level Project, and the Peoria and the World Project. Even though these projects are not exclusively social studies related, they should be heeded by persons contemplating change in the social studies.

Foxfire—Light One Candle

"Curriculum improvement," Chapter I aptly states, "does not have to be an all-fronts, full-scale attack all of the time. It can be as humble—though nonetheless important—as a single teacher or a small group of professionals with an idea worth developing." The Foxfire Project illustrates what the individual teacher is capable of doing within a classroom.[7]

The Foxfire Project, born in Rabun Gap, Georgia in 1966, resulted in a journal based on a variety of firsthand day-to-day living experiences as told by the people of that community. Eliot Wigginton, an English teacher at Rabun Gap High School, began the Foxfire Project by making students aware that as grandparents moved out of their lives, the grandparents took with them valuable and irreplaceable information.

Oral history recaptures the past through the oral recollections of those who experienced it firsthand. The rise of Foxfire-type projects, or cultural journalism, constitutes an important grassroots phenomenon within school curriculum. The number of projects is increasing rapidly. Lincoln King of the Loblolly Project in Gary, Texas, estimates that there are at least one hundred cultural journalism on-going projects in the United States today. This represents an innovation in school-community relations.

The Mendocino College Interdisciplinary Education Project— Getting Together Around an Idea

"Interdisciplinarity" at Mendocino College, California, is defined as (1) a focus on a thematic curriculum plan, (2) development of common curriculum goals which incorporate related disciplines, and (3) consistent planning and sequencing of instructional activities.[8]

The project was developed by a planning team representing the social and natural sciences and agriculture. To establish "interdisciplinarity," they first developed a set of goals around a selected theme, "World Food Crisis." This theme was selected because of student interest, the qualifications and interest of the staff, and the available resources.

The Mendocino College Interdisciplinary Education Project was born out of a need to serve two populations, the liberal arts student seeking an understanding of contemporary social issues, and the small landowner seeking practical skills for sustenance and single-family food production. The curriculum consisted of required "core" courses and electives. A workshop was planned for the students as the program's culminating event.

This thematic approach appears to have several advantages. It brought together students from diverse backgrounds and enhanced peer learning. It encouraged academics to re-evaluate course content and probably to think more in terms of student learning outcomes. Other schools considering team teaching or cross-disciplinary courses might well find the task easier if a theme of common interest is selected.

Adult Performance Level Project— What Do People Need To Know?

Curriculum reform can grow in a variety of garden spots. The Adult Performance Level Project may be unique because it was planned to "grow" in the real world of adult performance.[9] The project started with a random sampling investigation of today's adult population needs. It defined "functional literacy" as the ability to use skills and knowledge with the competence needed to meet the requirements of adult living. The project's purpose was to specify the competencies needed to achieve economic and educational success in today's society, and to develop assessment tools for American adults.

The procedure for identifying basic requirements for adult living was fourfold. First, related literature and research were reviewed to identify categories of needs of the undereducated and underemployed adult. Second, a survey of state and federal agencies and foundations was conducted to identify characteristics which distinguish successful from unsuccessful adults. Third, conferences on adult needs were conducted in various regions of the country to review study progress and to gather additional information. Last, interviews were conducted with undereducated and underemployed persons.

Adult needs were organized into "general knowledge areas." These areas are considered the content of adult literacy; they are consumer economics, occupational knowledge, community resources, health, and government and law. Four skill areas were also identified: communication skills (reading, writing, speaking, and listening), computation skills, problem-solving skills, and interpersonal relationship skills.

	CONSUMER ECONOMICS	OCCUPATIONAL KNOWLEDGE	HEALTH	COMMUNITY RESOURCES	GOVERNMENT AND LAW
READING	Reading a newspaper grocery ad				
WRITING	Writing a grocery list				
SPEAKING, LISTENING, VIEWING	Listening to an advertisement on the radio				
COMPUTATION	Computing the unit price of a grocery item		PERFORMANCE REQUIREMENTS		
PROBLEM SOLVING	Determining the best stores in which to shop				
INTERPERSONAL RELATIONS	Interacting with a sales clerk successfully				

The APL Model of Functional Competency

The staff of the project then developed a five-element methodology for curriculum development: specification of competencies, development of performance indicators, field testing and subsequent revision, national assessment of competency, and determination of competency levels. Employing the information gathered from these five steps, the project staff developed a grid pattern which allowed them to visualize how the various pieces of information could work together to provide a map for curriculum writing. Using this grid, classroom materials covering all the performance requirements of functional literacy were written. This scheme provided a quick overview of what needed to be done and allowed for systematic review.

The process used by this project is too expensive for a local district, but the theoretical model, a grid system, could be useful to all curriculum workers as a means of bringing about systematic improvement. The wider needs assessment phase is seldom done beyond even a single community. Curriculum change efforts are usually confined to individual classrooms or schools and fail to consider societal impact. The needs of the community and of society are as basic to curriculum planning, however, as the immediate needs of students. Several of the competency areas seem to fit logically in the social studies area.

Peoria and the World—Newspapers as a Resource

The Peoria, Illinois, school district addressed the issues of content and relevancy in school curriculum. Could students be motivated to know and care about the interdependence of the world? Sallie Whelan, Director of Education Services for the Peoria, Illinois *Journal Star*, and three teachers served on an advisory committee one summer to produce a teaching guide called *Peoria and the World*.[10] The newspaper teaching project was based upon the assumption that students could learn about the world by studying news concerned with Peoria and central Illinois. (In an article entitled " 'Peoria and the World' and [Your Town] and the World," in *Social Education*, Whelan discusses this approach to curriculum improvement.)

Interest and a willingness to use the newspaper for a global understanding already existed in the schools. James E. Becker, of the Social Studies Development Center at Indiana University, had worked with Peoria teachers several years before, and was familiar with their "Newspaper in the Classroom Program."

Because Becker remembered what the Peoria schools were doing, he sent them information on Chadwick F. Alger's project, "Columbus in the World/The World in Columbus."

The Peoria group was intrigued by Alger's point that people do not see the interdependent relationship between themselves and the rest of the world. With more information on the Mid-America program and with Becker's help, the advisory group in Peoria started to work. They clipped materials from the local paper, designed classroom lessons that could be integrated into almost every subject area and across different grade levels, and prepared the teaching guide.

In the fall, three teachers introduced the materials to their students. The awareness of a global perspective was extended by out-of-classroom activities, such as making a scrapbook to send to students in Saudi Arabia, writing letters to public officials, writing a student newspaper, and interviewing other fourth graders about the world community.

The flexibility of the materials designed may have been a key factor in teacher acceptance. Classroom lessons could be used in a variety of content areas, and different ability levels were considered, too. The materials could be integrated into the on-going curriculum with a minimum of disruption. Teachers did not have to revamp their course of study.

This case study suggests some elements that may increase the chances for successful curriculum improvement. First, the Peoria group were interested people who saw the need for curriculum change. Second, information and encouragement were available to teachers from other professional educators. Third, classroom teacher involvement in the development of materials facilitated the subsequent testing of the guide and materials in the teachers' classrooms.

This experience shows how change sometimes begins without complex plans, growing instead from the ideas and the involvement of a few individuals.

Generic Curriculum Change Models—
Taking the Best for Social Studies

Looking beyond social studies widens the horizon to focus on considerations which social studies educators need to keep in mind. The Esperanza Model, the Parent Involvement component of the project Follow Through, and the Urban-Rural Development Program provide valuable information.

The Esperanza Model attempts to convert a mono-cultural curriculum into a multicultural curriculum that recognizes the heritage and culture of minority groups. The Esperanza Model is apropos to the social studies curriculum because its goal is to develop an understanding of cultural pluralism. This model draws heavily from the social sciences to increase teacher awareness of the neglected history and culture of minority groups. The Parent Involvement component of project Follow Through is perhaps the leading example of how the school can involve parents. The Urban-Rural Development Project suggests an alternative for school systems that are geographically isolated from the resources needed for curriculum revision. Schools rarely have all the resources that would be helpful, but the sharing of the little wealth that is available may help.

The Esperanza Model— the Contributions of All People

The Esperanza Model presupposes that a mono-cultural curriculum should be enriched to provide self-actualizing experiences for the minority children and enrichment for the Anglo child as well.[11] The chart on page 54 shows the steps used to change a mono-cultural curriculum into a curriculum that values cultural pluralism. Each step entails specific activities leading toward the goal. The model moves from awareness to implementation. Apathy, complacency, tradition, and personal prejudices are candidly re-examined by participants using this model. The model employs techniques to encourage psychological insight and to help individuals evaluate where the curriculum is now. Then knowledge about cultural pluralism is provided so school personnel can reflect on where they want the curriculum to be in the future. The systematic nature of the Esperanza Model discourages curriculum reformers from attacking the problem in a haphazard manner.

The importance of eliminating racism from school curriculum cannot be overstated. Any school contemplating curriculum revision should incorporate the type of thoughtful reflection into the process which this model represents. To end up with a "new" curriculum which still ignores or stereotypes by sex or ethnic heritage is indefensible.

The Esperanza Model

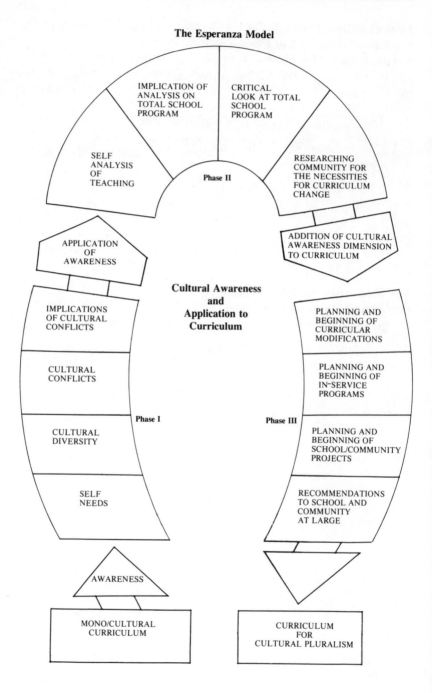

IMPLICATION OF ANALYSIS ON TOTAL SCHOOL PROGRAM

CRITICAL LOOK AT TOTAL SCHOOL PROGRAM

SELF ANALYSIS OF TEACHING

Phase II

RESEARCHING COMMUNITY FOR THE NECESSITIES FOR CURRICULUM CHANGE

APPLICATION OF AWARENESS

Cultural Awareness and Application to Curriculum

ADDITION OF CULTURAL AWARENESS DIMENSION TO CURRICULUM

IMPLICATIONS OF CULTURAL CONFLICTS

PLANNING AND BEGINNING OF CURRICULAR MODIFICATIONS

CULTURAL CONFLICTS

PLANNING AND BEGINNING OF IN-SERVICE PROGRAMS

Phase I

Phase III

CULTURAL DIVERSITY

PLANNING AND BEGINNING OF SCHOOL/COMMUNITY PROJECTS

SELF NEEDS

RECOMMENDATIONS TO SCHOOL AND COMMUNITY AT LARGE

AWARENESS

MONO/CULTURAL CURRICULUM

CURRICULUM FOR CULTURAL PLURALISM

**Project Follow Through—
the Parent Involvement Component—
Parents Count, Too**

The importance of parent involvement in the school is supported by a recent study conducted in Minnesota. Johnson's study, "Parents' Preferences for Educational Alternatives," questioned parents about the desirability of parental input into curriculum decisions.[12] The parents of 1,367 pupils responded to a questionnaire which allowed choices ranging from "school should decide with no advice from parents" to "parents should make final decision after advice from school."

In response to the question, "Should parents have a say regarding what courses of study are offered at their child's school?", sixty-one percent of the parents felt the school and parents should share the responsibility. Another item response, perhaps surprisingly to many, indicated the majority of parents also approved of student participation in curriculum decisions. Another item on the questionnaire even more strongly supported an active role for parents and students in curriculum change. When parents were asked "Who should decide what subjects your child actually studies in school?", over eighty percent responded that parents, children, and the school should decide cooperatively.

Follow Through is an example of a program that has incorporated parents directly into the schooling process.[13] It is a federally funded program focusing on kindergarten and primary grade children who were previously enrolled in Head Start or similar programs. Follow Through is designed to provide comprehensive services and parent participation activities that aid in the continuing development of children. Parents work on advisory committees, work as classroom volunteers or paid employees, receive home visits from project staff, and generally participate actively in the school programs. Communication between parents and the school is increased by home visits, letting parents know what is going on in the school, accompanying parents to schools, and sometimes being an advocate for parents at school or before social agencies.

The Los Angeles Follow Through Parent Involvement has an inservice training class that includes parents in the real planning of the program. These classes help teachers, teacher aides, support personnel, and parents to work as a team in meeting the academic, social, and cultural needs of children. According to project reports, greater parent involvement resulted in voluntary assistance in the classroom, better attendance at advisory council meetings, development of parent advisory council policy, planning of additional parent inservice classes, advisory assistance in curriculum planning, and participation in the development of curriculum and teaching aids.

The Father Organization is one component of the parent involvement plan in the Los Angeles City Unified School District.[14] This organization enables fathers to take an active role in their children's educational development. The aim is to provide for the much needed male role models in the elementary program.

This program illustrates how parental input is being incorporated at the early elementary level. As one approaches the intermediate and high school levels of instruction, there is a decrease in parental involvement. This situation might be remedied through an awareness of how Follow Through has succeeded in bridging the gap between the community and school, and through adequate adaptation.

Urban-Rural School Development Program— City Meets Country

Federal money was given to local school districts in the Urban-Rural School Development Program by the U.S. Office of Education.[15] This experiment in staff development was controlled by a local school-community council. The project's purpose was to help school districts design and implement innovative practices to improve their schools.

Geographic isolation proved to be a serious obstacle to the rural school districts. Materials and resources were often not available because of location. However, the schools attempted to compensate for a lack of local resources by inviting professors from other areas to visit for one- or two-day sessions. The rural sites then developed a university-affiliated, field-based professor program. The selected professor lived and worked in the area, teaching courses for school and community people and consulting regularly with district teachers.

Macon County, Georgia, and Wise County, Virginia, were the first rural areas to develop such programs. Program success resulted in the selection of four additional sites for similar programs: Crystal City, Texas; Hays/Lodge Pole, Montana; Bayfield, Wisconsin; and Louisville, Kentucky.

This experiment in staff development and curriculum review developed from a cooperative effort between the local schools and nearby universities. Together they decided the "experts" would be more valuable and knowledgeable as resident participants in the community. Bringing needed expertise to the community may make more sense than transporting school personnel to a university setting. Really being part of a community provides a different perspective.

Summary

Rather than summarize the summaries, we present the following chart (see pp. 58–59) to highlight some key points. Included are project titles, origin of change, intended audience, some selected strengths, and a small attempt at humor.

Drawing eclectically from these examples suggests some tentative truisms. Somebody has to care. The more persons who care, the better. This does not mean every teacher has to plan and be actively involved; however, keeping people informed and exposed to the goals and progress of curriculum improvement seems worthwhile. Solid knowledge about where the curriculum "is" never hurts. A consensus and commitment to where the curriculum should be going is worth the time it takes to avoid charging carelessly ahead. Time and money do not hurt, but much can be done with limited resources. Other curriculum efforts may not fit your community's needs exactly, but learning from others may help avoid mistakes. As social studies educators, recalling what we know about human behavior—such as the importance of effective leadership or how small groups can be task-oriented—should be helpful. Also, patience and preparedness can pay off; it may very well pay to light one little candle rather than to curse the darkness.

Summary Chart of "Curriculum Sampler"

Project or Model	Origin of Change	Intended Audience	Major Strengths
West Islip Schools— "Don't give up; good things are possible."	A single school district	School district Grades 4-6, teachers at grade level	Teacher involvement, needs assessment, evaluation model, publicity component
Social Studies Field Agent— "Experienced teachers should not just fade away."	A university	Local districts	Recognition of need for stable teacher population
Twin Cities Service Center— "Two or more pocketbooks are better than one."	Cooperation between districts	Individual teachers	Variety of ways to reach teachers, central location of resources
Development Economic Education Program—"Economists leave the ivory tower."	Professional academic society	Educators	Involvement of economists
Foxfire— "Grandmother goes to school."	Individual teacher	Classroom	Student interest, teacher involvement, community base, combination of skills, interdisciplinary
Mendocino College—"College professors can work together."	Team teaching effort	College classes in social and natural sciences and agriculture	Thematic appeal, team planning, student interest
Adult Performance Level Project—"The real world exists."	Nationwide federal funds	Adult population	Not tied to any single academic discipline, adaptability, systematic sampling of need

Project or Model	Origin of Change	Intended Audience	Major Strengths
Peoria and the World—"Reading beyond the comics."	Journalists and teachers	Peoria teachers	Cooperative effort, uses a neglected, inexpensive resource
Esperanza Model—"Racism's obituary."	A school district	All educators K-12	Societal need, systematic approach
Project Follow Through—"A neglected resource."	Nationwide federal funds	Schools and community, early elementary	Parental participation, community response
Urban-Rural Development—"Co-existence between country bumpkin and city slicker."	Federal funds, selected sites	School district	Cooperative approach, effective use of resources

Footnotes

[1]National Council for the Social Studies, *Social Studies Curriculum Guidelines: NCSS Position Statement*. Washington, D.C.: National Council for the Social Studies, 1971.

[2]*Social Studies Curriculum Materials Data Book*. Boulder, Colorado: Social Science Consortium, 1971.

[3]Andrew Adrian Pecorro, *The Installation of a Modern Social Studies Program in Grades Four–Six in the West Islip Public Schools*, unpublished dissertation. Nova University, December 1975.

[4]Gerald Marker and Howard D. Mehlinger, *Report of the Social Studies Field Agent Training Program*. Bloomington, Indiana: Indiana University, 1972.

[5]Jon R. Morris and James Olson, *A Formative Evaluation of the Twin Cities Area Social Studies Service Center*. St. Paul, Minnesota: Educational Research and Development Council, University of Minnesota, 1972.

[6]Joint Council on Economic Education, *Development Economic Education Program: Units and Bulletins*. New York: Joint Council on Economic Education, no date.

[7]Pamela Wood, *You and Aunt Arie*. Kennebunk, Maine: Star Press, Inc., 1975.

[8]Robert N. Wallen and Thomas F. MacMillan, "Interdisciplinary Education for Non-traditional Students: A Case Study in Change," paper presented to the

American Association of Community and Junior Colleges Annual Conference. Washington, D.C., 1976.

[9]Norvell, Northcutt, et al., *Adult Functional Competency: a Summary*. Austin, Texas: The University of Texas at Austin, Industrial and Business Training Bureau, 1975, p. 2a.

[10]Sallie Whelan, " 'Peoria and the World' and [Your Town] and the World," *Social Education*, January 1977, pp. 20–26.

[11]John Aragon, "An Impediment to Cultural Pluralism: Culturally Deficient Educators Attempting to Teach Culturally Different Children," unpublished paper presented at the El Paso Leadership Training Institute for Mexican American Educators, El Paso, Texas, 1972. (John Aragon is President of Highland University, Las Vegas, New Mexico.)

[12]Larry Johnson, "Parents' Preferences for Educational Alternatives," *The Elementary School Journal*, December 1975, pp. 165–169.

[13]Susan W. Rath, et al., *Follow Through: A Story of Educational Change*, Research Report, Office of Education. Washington, D.C.: Office of Education, Department of Health, Education and Welfare, 1976.

[14]Los Angeles City Unified School District, Project Follow Through, *Proposed Father Organization of Follow Through*, October 1974, pp. 91–93.

[15]Urban/Rural Leadership Training Institute, *Field-Based Teacher Education: Past, Present, and Future*. Stanford, California: SCRDT, Stanford University, 1975.

4
Help!
Who Can
and What Happens
When They Try?

Nancy W. Bauer

Why Is This Chapter Needed?

We have recently come to the end of a period of social reform in which the people who had the best education and the most advantages tried to help others to have the same. Political reform and educational reform financed by government were seen as ways of completing the American Dream. Government would legislate or adjudicate everyone's rights, and consultants from education would teach people how to use their rights for their own and society's good.

This has been the era of the consultant. Most people who have had success in some aspect of education have been called upon to share their experience with others. The assumption has been that experience shared can prevent repetition of mistakes and can transfer insights and success to others. People with experiences in the field and people who have derived models from their and other people's experiences have indeed been considered the "best and the brightest" and have been called upon to transfer their experience and their models to others.

NANCY W. BAUER is Adjunct Associate Professor, Graduate School of Education, University of Pennsylvania. She is a curriculum designer, textbook author, and consultant to schools in curriculum and staff development.

There has been a good deal of shared good will and a good deal of frustration for both the client and the consultant. To the client, the consultant sometimes seems to start too far down the road. Some consultants, on the other hand, begin at such an elementary level that the clients feel the consultants will never get to their concerns. From the consultants' point of view, it seems as if the clients hardly ever read the literature, or—if they do— why don't they believe it? Consultants feel that schools get on bandwagons that no longer are supported by research. Why is it that every one of us seems to have repeated the same cycle of decision-making? Schools start programs that research would be more than skeptical of. Why is it that so many school systems seem to have to rediscover the wheel?

Today it is time to evaluate why we do not always get the most for our money and how we might capitalize on our strengths. In this chapter we will look at users of consultants and then at the consultants themselves. Since the relationship between the two is reciprocal, each needs to know how that relationship looks to the other half of it. We will examine the ingredients of success and the reasons why some of the best efforts of both consultants and clients go awry. And finally, we will look at the politics of inservice training in which the consultants to school systems and their clients exist. The conclusions drawn at the end of the chapter will highlight the threads of success which run through all of these perspectives.

Who Calls In Outsiders?

Anyone who has been on one consulting assignment knows that a key question is "Who called me in?" In the minds of the teachers the consultant is tied to the sponsor. The position of that person who is the sponsor in the school district is crucial to the success of the consulting assignment.

Consultants learn quickly to be wary. Sometimes a consultant is called in by insiders who were once leaders but have now lost their constituency. These ex-leaders often hold onto their titles, but they must rely too heavily on them to get their colleagues to accept their direction. Bernard Baruch, speaking on political leadership, said, "Every time you use your authority you've lost some of it"; and "If you wish to be a political leader, look over your shoulder from time to time. If you can no longer see the people, you are no longer a political leader."

Too frequently consultants arrive in school districts to find out that they have been invited by someone who has either not looked over his or her shoulder recently or, when he or she last looked, could barely find the followers. It is even worse to be the invited guest of someone who has had to rely on such painful sayings as "I'm the Supervisor and responsible for the curriculum in this district. The teachers and the curriculum committees must carry out my policies." Or "I have been in this field for 25 years, and I understand what people ought to do and what they need to know." These are the verbal signals of a gap between Supervisor and teachers.

The particular consulting trap—i.e. helping the local leader who is royally disliked by all the teachers in the district—has appeared in recent years in many forms. There are *those with an axe to grind*. They have already picked out a textbook, a particular curriculum project, and a particular teaching skill; and they invite the consultant to come and tell the others that they are right.

Another kind or variation of this is a more grass-roots kind of trap. There are *teachers under pressure* by the school board or by a group of parents who read *The Saturday Review* and the Sunday *New York Times*. In self-defense they ask for a consultant to come and "tell us about the new social studies." Any consultant who has fallen for this ruse remembers lecturing for an hour about "the structure of the disciplines," or "a conceptual line," or "a process approach," or "an inquiry method," or "values dilemmas" (and all the other buzz words of that era). What followed was the question period in which the consultant became the object of the local vivisection league. The first question after a speech about "the new curriculum" is always a version of "What's the matter with the way we've been doing it?" This can be a devastating question, reflecting the fact that audiences who listen to consultants are often full of worry, sprinkled with a little guilt. The questions show that teachers most often know what their weaknesses are, so that when they ask about "what's new" they are really asking (or fishing to find out) if "what's new" will force them to tackle the problems they have never been able to solve.

The first lesson that is learned by consultants who survive an invitation either from leaders who have no followers or from worried teachers is:

Discover the strengths of the group and build on those. It is the only way to establish rapport in a short period of time and to be honest about the fact that we all have strengths and we all have weaknesses. The future should be built by identifying our strengths and going on from there.

Who else calls in consultants from the outside? There is throughout the nation a network of people who enjoy trying what is new and being the first to bring ideas into their school systems. They call themselves *"innovators,"* and they are the first to go to a new workshop or read a new book on curriculum practices (not usually on theory or research); and they often band together at regional and national meetings. Being an innovative teacher is one thing. Many of these "innovators" are teachers themselves, or were. Being a self-conscious "innovator" and a leader of a school or district is something else.

The innovators who make dangerous leaders are those who tend to look down upon teachers who are not so quick to pick up something new or who do not have their particular courage in a classroom. Just as they label themselves "innovators," or "innovative," they label the others "traditional," as if that were a bad word. Some of these people make up the group just discussed—the leaders who have lost their constituency. Some are tolerated by the majority of their fellow teachers as long as they do what they do for their own students and do not try to force anyone else to do them too. Some are just left alone by teachers to write curriculum guides which teachers quietly ignore.

This nationwide clique of innovators is often perpetuated in a chicken-and-egg way by those professors in departments of education who themselves overemphasize methodology or classroom gimmickry, giving too little attention to the application of subject matter, the uses of research about children, or questions of the relationship of philosophy to practice.

The latest bandwagon in the department of education finds its way to the state legislature and then to the popular press, the school board, or parent pressure groups. Therefore, it is not totally the fault of the innovators that they find themselves so far away from being democratic leaders in their school districts. Often they are forced to come up with something new just to perpetuate the jobs that they hold as department heads or curriculum supervisors. There is great pressure to justify one's salary by doing something new or different, rather than by getting better at what you already do or by helping others do what they do better.

It is not to deride people who take easily to innovation that they are pointed out. It is, however, to recognize that innovators often make better gadflies than they do leaders. A problem for the district with an innovator-leader is that one important role that needs to be played in the school district may be forgotten. That is the role of *integrating innovation into the general curriculum and making it possible, therefore, for the rest of the staff to build on their own strengths.* An excited innovator who is frustrated and angry at people who do not accept the latest idea and will not "try anything" often fails to distinguish between people of sound judgment who reject a particular change and ego-weak individuals who reject change out of a desperate fear of failure. No one wants to take unnecessary risks in front of the children (which is—one must admit—the world's worst place to fail).

Unless we are going to have a teaching profession made up only of ego-strong individuals who can afford to try anything in front of the children, those consultants and users of consultants who are responsible for leadership must recognize that lecturing to people on how not to be afraid, or how the new item is going to be thrilling to try, or how what is new is so much better than what worked yesterday, is not the kind of leadership that is going to help an entire school system or the majority of the students. This method of evangelical excitement or of derision of those who are not excited tends to lead the innovators to talk only to each other. These are the people of whom the old hands of a school system say, "Don't worry. They'll go away and I'll still be here long after they've gone." Much money and much heartache is spent as innovators' good ideas are lost, the excitement is dissipated, and frustration and anguish take the place of honest, cooperative progress and professional development.

What Kinds of Outsiders Are There? Some Pros and Cons

There are the subject matter outsiders. These are usually college professors from liberal arts departments, each one of whom is a specialist in one aspect of one of the disciplines for which social studies is responsible. The advantage in choosing such a consultant is that the information the district gets about interpretations of history or the particular usefulness of sociology or psychology or economics is likely to be up-to-date and clear-cut.

The difficulties in using such subject matter specialists are inherent both in the nature of their specialty and in the perspectives and motivation of some individuals. No card-carrying scholar can be an expert in all of American history from 1607 to the present day, or all of Asian studies, or all of the eighteenth century in Europe, or all of Latin America or Africa. The users of such consultants have to know how to turn that information into courses that deal with the entire sweep of American studies in an interdisciplinary mode. International studies have to be made cross-cultural, as well as cross-time and cross-space.

Choosing a subject matter consultant then becomes a matter of finding the common ground; i.e., selecting the person who sees his or her subject matter from a point of view which is applicable to the general education of the rest of us. The most helpful subject matter specialists are those who are philosophically concerned about the human race and see their particular subject matter as one of the places where that concern is applicable. They are also people who have personal interests beyond their own narrow area of specialization, are widely read, and are willing to talk and speculate (as well as worry and hope) beyond the area of their specialty.

A philosopher-scholar who cares about human beings and about general education of American citizens is often a better consultant than one whose own subject matter is too broad and too thin. The in-depth research scholar who works at the frontier in some way has more humility, is more careful of the uses of the evidence, and draws conclusions with less flamboyance than those who only use the scholarship of other people.

A subject matter specialist probably cannot create a curriculum for children. However, the well trained, active, subject matter specialist who cares about children and about the world can be enormously helpful to a school system which needs to know, for example, how the revolution in America, or the traditional Chinese family, or the impact of Britain on Africa fits into the major themes and questions which concern all of us.

Other helpful consultants to a well prepared school system are *the application specialists*. These are often professors in the schools of education who are not themselves subject matter specialists but have had experience of their own and experience in helping other school systems discover what can be used, by whom it can be used, and how that information can be made available to teachers and students. These individuals, if they are skilled in doing as well as in knowing, can use the techniques of teaching that engender participation and discussion as they work with the clients in the school system.

It is important to avoid those "how to" specialists who simply write or talk at the marketplace without knowing how to do it themselves. These people are often glib and even entertaining, but the frustration level of teachers who are left with having to "do it themselves" on Monday morning can cause a backlash that is turned on the curriculum, rather than on the perpetrator of the easy answers.

One of the great advantages of using people who are skilled in application comes when you find that you have chosen one who reads widely in the research literature on child development and also keeps up at least one subject matter interest in history and social science. There is no way to equate consultants who read a lot with those who do not read at all.

Other practitioners, supervisors, and teachers from other school districts can make excellent consultants. There is nothing like the comfort of working with people who have "been there." They are less likely to offer such wonderful instructions as "Hold a discussion," or "You will want to role-play this situation," or "You will want to have one of the parents come to class to tell the children what it is like to travel to Antarctica."

On the other hand, the practitioner who is totally wrapped up in the unit of instruction which he or she has developed and which has been taught in a particular way in his or her classroom is often unable to generalize beyond that individual experience. Without a theoretical base, there may be no follow-up. Theory is needed in order to build new examples or modify the original one.

Many practitioners and application specialists fall into the trap of offering "models" for teachers to follow. No teacher who teaches 35 students a day in many subjects, or 180 a day in one subject, has the time or probably the expertise to take that model and use it for the preparation of new units of study and new lessons, or for the gathering of new material.

There is a category of outsiders who can be enormously helpful because of their information about the politics of curriculum change and the financing of curriculum improvement. These are *the state-wide supervisors in each of the subject matter areas and their staffs*. When these people speak in their area of expertise, they can prevent a great deal of failure and can offer practical help in how to improve the chances for success of a new program. They can also be helpful in the selection of subject matter specialists, application specialists, and teacher practitioners from other school districts. What are to be avoided are the state consultants who fall into the category of the network of innovators or are simply demonstration teachers who show one particular classroom trick which is usable by some (but if so, only for a minute).

Other useful sources for consulting services are *the publishers' representatives*. They have the advantage of being constantly interested in whether the actual program continues to work in the five classrooms every day of the week. The publishers are not able to put the blame for failure on a theory, or the motivation of the teachers, or the background of the children. Their stockholders are only concerned with the satisfied customer; therefore, publishers' representatives tend to listen very carefully. They take great risks, and they try to minimize those risks by accurate information and the most conservative estimates of the possible.

The publishers' representatives are usually of three kinds. There is the sales representative who most often was a teacher or a school principal or a department head and has since become part of the business side of the organization. These people are enormously helpful in spotting trouble and in calling in aid.

Publishers also have full-time consultants who are themselves successful classroom teachers, often of the innovative variety. These are the people who are used to "winging it" and can do demonstration lessons any time, any place, with any group of children, even if the textbooks have failed to arrive from the warehouse. These people can "present" a program and highlight the helpful features. They can also diagnose what is causing the gap between the promises of the features of a program and the program in actual practice. Is it because one of the features is not working? Or is it because the teachers, no matter what they say, are simply not using that particular feature and therefore are not achieving the desired result? A consultant of this kind is best used both at the beginning of the use of a new program and again three or four months later, when a number of people have committed themselves to it and have tried to give it their best.

There are some publishers who can supply authors and editors who were responsible for the creation of the product in the first place. These people vary greatly in their helpfulness, depending on their ego-strength and sense of humor. There is only one thing worse than the pride of an author and that is the pride of an editor. It takes a great deal of experience for those responsible for creating a product to be able to realize that it has a life of its own and that it can be a great improvement on what was there, without necessarily being the last word for every person everywhere. Not every author or editor ought to be used as a consultant. Those who have had classroom experience, supervisory experience, an in-depth academic background, and enough perspective to have a sense of humor are those who can be of greatest help.

Who Uses Outsiders Most Effectively?

The people who get the most out of their consultants and provide the best curriculum leadership for their schools and school districts are those who, among themselves, have taken the time and the interest in each other to agree on their common needs and on their common agenda. There is much work to be done within a school district by both the policy-makers, the supervisors, and the teachers before they are ready to choose and use a consultant wisely.

Knowing what it is that the parents and the educators and the political leaders collectively or cumulatively want for the children and agreeing to try to meet all of those felt needs is a first step. Although everyone's "felt need" is not equally valid or even good for children, every well-meaning adult in the children's lives deserves to be heard. The needs then must be matched against the research. Is it possible for children at a particular age to accomplish those things which the adults have in mind? Is it possible or probable that the methodology people would like to see practiced with the children is going to be effective? Is it possible that teachers who are generally well trained can carry out a new mandate without careful consideration of where and how what is new will be fitted into or "infused" into what is now being accomplished?

School districts and all the people who hope to influence them have an enormous job to do in keeping up with what is known by others. Once they have decided what they would like to do or accomplish and they have subtracted from that what they already know, or think they know, and have corroborated it by reading in the research and reading about other people's experiences, then the school district has a realistic assessment of "knowing what they don't know." The most effective people in any field are those who are knowledgeable, open to learning from experience, and aware of what they do not know.

A school district needs to know where to get help to fill in the gaps in its own knowledge or experience. The call to a consultant is most successful when the clients have determined their questions in common. If the clients do not know what the common questions are, then the outside consultant must spend the first part of the job determining those questions. Common questions can be quite broad, such as: How can one build what is known about child development into our K-12 reading or social studies program? How can one build a K-12 program of writing skills? How can one build a K-12 program in social studies which will enhance the possibility that all children will be able to deal with the concept of time and the concept of space? What are ways in which history and social science can be integrated into our interdisciplinary social studies in the one or two periods a day which the school district has allotted to us? The positive signs that the outside consultant looks for are the goals and questions that come from insiders who talk to each other.

Another group successful in using help is one in which the leaders (representatives of the school board, the superintendent, the principal, and the department heads) "take the training" with the staff. There is nothing more disheartening to a consultant than to be introduced by the person who holds the political responsibility and the political leadership in the district, and hear him say to the teachers, "I know you will enjoy your day with Dr. Blank and that you will work hard because he has so much to teach you. I am sorry that I cannot be with you, but I have a very important meeting that I must attend; but I wish you well." The wise consultant who also wields enough power is one who insists, as a condition of agreeing to take on the job, that the superintendent take the principal's workshop and the principal take the teacher's workshop, and, wherever possible, some representatives to the board of education be participants.

A corollary to this criterion of participation from the top is that the group have a plan ready for acting upon the results of the consultant's workshop. Before the consultant is brought in, there ought to be a definite statement of need; after the consultant goes, there ought to be a definite plan for utilizing the results. The presence of the line officer who holds the responsibility for making and carrying out the policies is an indication that the district takes the goals, the consultantship, and the staff seriously, and that no one is wasting his or her time.

Those who keep a flexible plan are also likely to get the most from the use of an outsider. To plan policy and goals and some criteria in advance and to leave them flexible until the consultant has done his or her work is only sensible. Otherwise the consultant has simply been hired to "fill in the blank" or to answer such off-target questions as "How can we get Japan into the fourth grade?" The district's plan should include an accurate assessment of what fourth graders on the whole can be expected to do and what resources are available to accomplish that goal. The consultant and the staff are then free to examine critically what subject matter or content areas best suit that particular slot in the curriculum. Being "on Japan" is not a curriculum goal. Even if the school district decides to "do Japan" in the fourth grade, a more important question would be, "Why are we doing Japan? And what do we expect the students to get out of it?"

What Kinds of Insiders Are There?

It is often not necessary to go outside the school district for consultants, although the advantage to doing so is that, first of all, the outsider looks like an expert and, secondly, he or she is not involved in the politics of the day-to-day working of the school system. An outsider can say things more boldly and, using the skills of group dynamics, can often help the various groups within a system who must work together to talk through their common responsibility and their individual frustrations. It is also helpful, as with any outside "clinician," to recognize that what is the matter in one district has really happened in 500 others and that it is perfectly normal to be going through the problems they are going through. "There is a lot of this going around."

When are insiders most helpful? Once a sense of direction has been set, a philosophy and policy have been adopted, and the types of materials which will carry out those policies have been selected, it is often better to use consultants from "home" rather than outsiders, or perhaps a combination of the two.

The advantages of the insiders are that they see much of the detail and can work within the limitations of the particular resources of the district. They also can be helpful in a continuing way, particularly if they really believe they are sharing what they know with colleagues, rather than telling the handicapped what to do. Everyone has something to offer and something to learn. There are no permanent helpers, nor those permanently in need of help.

Supervisors in subject matter areas are particularly helpful as inside consultants as long as they realize that they are part of a cooperative venture. They are really staff people who take a great deal of responsibility, but who share the authority with those who are in the classroom, as well as with the parents in the community. This is a very difficult task. Supervisors need to know a great deal more than the persons with whom they work, yet they must have honest respect for the people they are hired to help. Supervisors can benefit from training in group dynamics and democratic leadership.

But how to avoid post-consultant lag? With all the good will in the world and all the years of preparation and all the cooperation among the members of the school district before the consultant comes and all the careful attention to both theory and practice during the consulting session, the moment of truth does come. The evangelist goes home. The Hawthorne Effect is over, and the school district is on its own.

The support system must be in place by the time the consultant leaves, or most of the good withers away. To give the recommendations continuing momentum, there must be both philosophical commitment and policy statements at the district level and the money to support and implement that commitment. Money is needed both for materials and for a time for teachers to meet and work together with each other and with parents to think through, work through, talk through, and practice what it is they are going to do. They need time to meet periodically as the program continues in order to share their moments of triumph and their hours of frustration when theory meets practice and the variations that are going to be needed become more and more obvious. If it is worth the time and money and effort to develop goals and objectives and to bring in consultants to help, then it seems only obvious that there should be time and money and philosophical commitment to go on and help make whatever it is they have decided to do a success. Much educational money and much educational momentum are lost when programs are launched and then left to flounder. There is no program, no teaching strategy, no curriculum guide, and no social studies textbook that can flourish without grass-roots support.

Who Has a Right To Be a Consultant?

Consultants have to be honest with themselves about the breadth and depth of their own experience and their own expertise. There is a euphoria that comes with being a successful consultant, causing an occasional reluctance to give up one's following when that particular expertise is no longer in fashion. Then there is the disease which causes the consultant to stay on one track and continue to push a single idea. The first symptom of this is the overused Ph.D. dissertation. Some consultants seem unwilling to go back and rethink what they know, what other people need, and where they may have been well-meaning in the past but not as helpful as they might have been.

There is, in addition, the disease of omniscience—being an expert on everything. Particularly in this era of highly specific, sometimes narrow approaches to curriculum (which are often sponsored by government grants for a particular "finger-in-the-dike" need), one is surprised to find the same names appearing as consultants on career education, economic education, reading, child development, moral development, and citizenship. When a new bandwagon appears, one hopes the skilled consultant will work to get that vehicle into the mainstream of traffic, rather than just ride it while it is popular. A good consultant continues to read and to work with new partners in order to know enough to help.

Before consultants dare to give advice to others, they need to be aware of and totally open about their own standards. Standards of excellence—in teaching, in academic scholarship, in understanding the country, in wanting students to be citizens, in concern for democratic philosophy—should not and must not change from client to client. The clients have a right to know ahead of time where consultants stand and what kinds of high standards they hold. Clients do not need consultants who adjust their standards to the school district. In such cases the client district never finds out where it is on a nationwide scale. Strategies for helping, however, should change from client to client.

The major benefit of outside consultants is that they have been to other school districts and can compare one with another. They should know what are the normal ranges of teaching and parenting, and the various stages that children go through. Consultants need to commit themselves to a considerable amount of travel and a considerable amount of continuing observation. One cannot continue to be a viable consultant based on memories of times past from 10 or 15 or 20 years ago.

If the consultant has wide experience as well as recent experience, then it is possible to analyze a situation in a district and recognize what the actual causes of a problem may be and what the strengths of the district really are, and help the staff to minimize its problems and make the most of its strengths. Helpful consultants are the ones who have a storehouse of information and experience, but wait until they arrive on site before deciding exactly what they are going to recommend. They do not give canned advice from district to district.

In order to help, a consultant must be able to identify with the clients. Or, as this writer was told many years ago by Ronald Lippitt, "You have to learn to love the people whose values you may hate." It is absolutely necessary to recognize the clients' rights to their own insights, feelings, perspectives, and limitations. One has to be willing to learn from them. Perhaps their fears or their hang-ups can teach the consultant what the real barriers to improvement are. One must never look with disdain upon honest fears or honest inability to mobilize for change.

One of the problems in some school districts is that they invite a whole battery of well known consultants. Each is supposed to come and "say something," but is not required to coordinate his or her efforts. Where school districts do wish to vary the consulting talent available, they should try to supply all the consultants with information about what the others are doing and also give them an overall picture of the preparation the school system has made before the consultants arrive.

Consultants Talk to Themselves

Whether you are a user of consultants, a consultant yourself, or both, it is important to understand how consultants think and operate. In this section, each reader is asked to think like a consultant and view the situation from the consultant's perspective. Consultants talk to themselves a great deal. If one is going to be a consultant, dialogue with oneself is absolutely necessary in order to be as helpful as possible and as realistic as possible, and still to keep one's standards high. The dialogue focuses around two major questions.

Where will they be when I leave? This question is crucial in order to set realistic targets. There are many traps in consulting, but the worst one is to begin giving advice before listening to the client. To set realistic targets so that everyone knows at the beginning where the consultant expects to be when the session is over, the consultant has to know where the client is at the beginning.

If a consultant is invited to start the consulting session at 9 o'clock in the morning, then he or she should have breakfast with some of the clients. If the consultant has that worst-of-all-possible-hours—3:15 in the afternoon—he or she should be sure to wander around as people drift in and collapse in the back row. The consultant should introduce himself or herself and ask them why they are there and what could happen to make this a successful session for them; and then suggest, as trial balloons, some of the things that he or she may wish to bring up. It is in this way that the consultant discovers the gap between the reasons why people came and the reasons why the people who invited the consultant did the inviting. It is important to know ahead of time what that gap is. Shooting galleries are fun, but being the target is not a pleasant role to play.

People who attend workshops are most concerned with what they are going to do on Monday morning. To focus on that concern a consultant must find out what those practical worries are, what teachers feel are their greatest strengths, and what works best with their students. Teachers will gladly tell the consultant, if asked. Only with this information can a consultant help to provide continuity between where they are and where they wish to go, or where the consultant thinks they ought to go.

If it is not possible to have a relaxed, informal session for even ten or fifteen minutes before the consultant begins, then it is almost better to have the question period first. In such a prologue-question period, the consultant can ask, "Where do you want to be when this is over?" and "Why are you here?" (The answer to that is sometimes devastating, such as, "The rest of the faculty took the third grade to the zoo, so I had to come.") The beginning is also the time to find out whether the boss is in the group and what roles each of the people plays. It is a terrible trap to talk about the particular participants in a school system and not know that they are right there in one's workshop.

How can the district help the consultant to work best with the time limitations that exist? This is an important question to answer in order to make the best use of the time one has without overloading the session with everything one knows. Whatever the topic, there must be time for the participants to help in the initial analysis, and time for feedback on how they feel about possible solutions. A speech can take half an hour. A speech and discussion should take an hour and a half at the most. But a workshop in which the targets are clear and there is genuine participation takes a block of time, at least three hours. The number of people involved is not so important as determining how best to work within time limits.

In addition to considering the two haunting questions, experienced consultants and their clients will recognize five mottos.

1. *All models require raw materials to make them work, or they become dogmatic.* Theoretical models (e.g., how to build a concept; how to build a values dimension or a philosophical element into the curriculum; how to use subject matter disciplines for specific objectives at particular grade levels) all require a great deal of understanding and easy availability of raw materials.

There is serious doubt that a consultant can use theory effectively with teacher practitioners unless they have for their daily use a curriculum plan and materials which make the theoretical models possible for use in their classrooms. If a school district is in the process of developing its own curriculum guidelines, it still must have available the money and time to collect and analyze the raw materials through which the theory will come alive in a classroom. Theory without practice and theory without actual materials become dogma, just memorized catch words and phrases that have very little effect on the actual teaching in the classroom. This is what has happened to a great many theories, including Dewey's, Taba's, Piaget's, and Kohlberg's.

Knowing the theory is enormously helpful, but unless the practitioner also knows the raw materials out of which the theory was built, the theoretical models can become dogma. When new raw materials come to life, the dogmatic practitioner is unable to test the theoretical models with the new evidence, the new facts, the new classroom situation, or the new subject matter. When theories are left untested, they are applied where they no longer should be, or they are not revised when they might be. Much good theory dies from rigid application.

2. *Interdisciplinary approaches take more discipline.* Consultants also mutter to themselves when new subject matter is to be introduced into the curriculum. There are always new subject matters as we become more and more mobile in our understanding and more and more introspective as a society. We need to know America in much greater depth than we ever understood it before, and we also need to know much more about other cultures and their politics and economics. What does a consultant do?

First of all, a consultant has to know a great deal about the subject matter and the curriculum. Either the new information has to be worked into the current curriculum or the curriculum has to be adjusted because it can no longer accommodate the insights of the new subject matter. Consultants also need to have been experts at some time in their life on something, so that they can recognize when the new subject matter is being treated in an academically valid fashion and not just in a superficial one. Consultants also have their consultants (like a Federal Reserve Bank for scholarship). It is important for a consultant to be able to call on qualified research scholars to find out what they know, so that weaving the new material and new insights into the curriculum will not distort the scholarship. Recently, a university professor groaned when he described his best student from his course in American Civilization, who, after graduating, had gone on to teach at a local high school and who had come back to tell the professor that "I'm teaching the course to these kids just the way you taught it to me, and it's working beautifully." Obviously, the student did not know enough about the field to be able to pick and choose and reorder the elements of the subject for the needs of a high school class. The college course was based on the assumption that a student had had a solid grounding in the great themes, ideas, and important events of American history. The student, now turned teacher, had ignored the responsibility of giving the high school students their introductory course and,

instead, was teaching them their second one. Granted, it is difficult to take only those insights from the new course that can be
understood "the first time around" and leave behind all those
joyous moments which the advanced student had so delighted
in.

So it is with consultants. They must continue to be students
and at the same time realize that their main job in the subject
matter area is to help find some interdisciplinary ways to bring
new learning to students, ways that are consonant with their
own cognitive and emotional development.

3. *Fragments don't weave in. Infuse, integrate, or forget it.*
Not since Current Events Friday has a fragment made it into
social studies. Materials do not paste on or plug in. Important
ways of looking at the world—like those involving environmental education, economic education, career education, law-fo-
cused education—or topics like drug education and sex education, do not last as subject matter when they are added on or
dropped in. It is like adding another egg to the cake after it has
been baked. It simply is never part of the original and not very
digestible. And people don't try it again.

New or renewed emphases are important, but they need to be
woven into the total curriculum fabric. One of the reasons why
some textbooks continually win out over consultants' advice is
that every time a textbook is revised, new information has a
chance of being properly placed. Old information can be given
different emphasis. Where textbooks simply plug in all the new
features in order to accommodate the new pressures, it is not
only obvious to the eye but it is also very difficult to teach. If the
consultants or the authors of the books cannot figure out how the
new materials relate day-by-day to the old materials, how is the
teacher who is on the line without the time, the background, or
the energy supposed to be able to do it?

Innovative ideas are extremely important to the health of education in our democracy, but we need to provide the climate
which will make those new ideas connect to the old ones and
help those new ideas develop with sound standards and workable plans. Then they will have every chance to succeed.

Insiders and outsiders alike need to set up criteria for new
emphases and ideas. Is the scholarship sound? Are materials
really available that are useful in reaching that goal with children
in that age-range? Is evaluation possible? Once all of those ques-

tions are answered, teachers can be helped to figure out how to incorporate the new ideas into the work that is already being done, without losing the value of all that has been done in the past. In this way, new ideas can flourish, bringing long-term growth.

4. *Pilot projects rarely spread.* One of the things we learned in the era of the big money and the big projects is that pilot projects in school districts where there is no philosophical commitment to the goals and no policy commitment to the success of the program are relatively useless. Even if the pilot is successful in the one school or two schools in which something is being tried, other schools seldom follow. A successful pilot in another building (or even in another classroom) can cause others to be afraid to try for fear they might not do as well. If, on the other hand, the pilot has a weak beginning, it may be rejected without giving it the opportunity to be helped and strengthened and built into a sizeable success.

It is understandable that school districts do not want to spend a lot of money or spend a lot of good will on a new direction without having carefully thought it through and tried it out. The usefulness of the pilot comes after the school district has committed itself to particular goals, such as more language experience associated with reading in social studies, or more understanding of the dynamics of contacts between bigger and smaller nations.

Once the goals of a school district have been set, then to have several pilots try different ways of reaching those goals makes very good sense. Each pilot will have behind it people who are committed to the success of the goals. They will test the method or materials rather than simply try to defeat them. The competition is aimed at reaching the goals in the most efficient and interesting way. It may even be possible to adopt more than one way of reaching the goals. But to have competing pilots whose philosophies and methodologies are totally different is to put the pilots into a leaderless situation.

5. *Demonstration lessons don't win friends.* Anyone who has ever completed a successful demonstration lesson knows what is meant by this maxim. All consultants have enjoyed the heady success of watching a group of children whom they have never seen before fall all over themselves to delight in everything the consultant tries to do—in front of their teachers who have to

struggle with them every day. There should always be a tape recorder at the door on the way out to record the comments of the teachers, such as, "Well, if she only had *my* kids" or "I'd like to see her try that at one o'clock in the afternoon after it's been raining for five days, and there's been no recess."

The demonstration lessons that really sell people on trying them themselves are the ones which fail and thereby make the consultant look more like a human being and less like a guru. All consultants have experienced failure in front of an audience of 75 adults watching them teach 35 children badly. There is one redeeming feature to a poor demonstration. Sometimes what doesn't work is an enormously helpful base for working together with the clients to try to do a better job.

The Politics of Inservice

The consultant-client relationship in schools exists in a political context which often puts pressure on the agenda. Because education is both a profession and a public service, the professional staff in curriculum development must be responsive to the concerns (and sometimes the demands) of citizens and their legislative representatives.

These concerns often skew the agenda. Although they should be discussed and should be considered important by the professionals in their working relationships, the problem lies in the desire of the professionals to respond to the public and respond rapidly. Responding rapidly to outside pressure can cause knowledgeable professionals to ignore the criteria for successful needs assessment, long-range building of relationships among personnel, and development of standards for total curriculum and staff development. The agenda can become skewed when the consulting sessions focus too soon on issues such as accountability, competency-based education, and statewide or national assessment of students.

Inservice work which involves teachers, supervisors, and the leaders of the school district does occur in a political setting, because public education in a democracy is and, indeed, ought to be a political matter. The concerns of the public must be considered within a realistic assessment by the school district of what it can actually deliver. To promise everything that the citizens want for their children is ridiculous. Teachers, school districts, and their consultants need to know the ingredients of success that are possible within the limitations of the school setting and to use all the ingredients of success, indeed to demand them. When known ingredients of success are withheld from the school district because of money or lack of support of the administration, the school board, or the state, teachers should speak up about that, too. It is hoped that professional organizations will increasingly speak out for what is known in the field. Together, outside consultants, inside administrators, teachers, parents, and legislators could work realistically toward the best of all possible goals.

What Does It Take: An Inner View

The discussion of consultants—who can be one and who can use one best—is actually a discussion of educational goals and how to make the most of them. As in most worthwhile ventures, an improving educational climate is characterized by some inner assumptions.

Optimism is one of these, because it is the optimistic view of human nature that makes adults trust each other to be helpful as they trust the children to be educable. Education is an optimistic venture based on a view of human nature as basically good (or at least doing its damnedest). Without such an optimistic view of the entire educational process, inservice training and consultant help are just manipulations of fixed conditions to shift the power or minimize the pain in a basically hopeless situation. People who believe in the future must believe in each other and in the ability of all of us to become stronger by pooling our resources, our insights, and our experiences.

Realism is another of the inner views. It keeps optimism from being simply a flight of fancy. Realistic optimists are those who know what is possible for a particular age-range of children; what is known from other people's experience and research about the easiest and cheapest ways to get where we want to go; and what constitutes expertise, who has it, and how to get it to help in a particular situation. Optimistic realists use all the resources they can get toward the goals that are worth working for.

Because it operates in a realistic setting and because we are always startlingly far from where we wish we were, the entire education venture is conditioned by a sense of humor. There is something delightfully funny about cockeyed optimists working toward an increasingly perfectible, humane, and workable world through the sometimes ridiculous conditions we have perpetrated upon ourselves.

It takes a sense of humor to be ego-strong enough to ask for help without fear. It takes ego-strength to give help without arrogance. Optimistic realists with a sense of humor know when and how to get help and can put that help to good use in the best of all possible life works—the improvement of the human condition through the development of competent and humane children.

5

Library Resources To Support Curriculum Improvement

Jack W. Miller and Edward V. Johnson

Ray Muessig opened this Bulletin with some Robert Benchley humor, a "List of Points Related to Curriculum Improvement," and examples of the varied educational needs and desires that can be manifest within a single community. Multiply Muessig's "Excelsior Public Schools" situation by perhaps fifty thousand, and you begin to see the heterogeneity of public and private education in the United States. Social studies programs in American elementary and secondary schools are as remarkable for their individuality and diversity as for the common elements shared among them. Repeated attempts have been made over the past four decades to "correct" this situation and impose a relatively standard scope and sequence from school to school, district to district, and state to state. These reports and projects have enjoyed very limited success and, if anything, have tended to further broaden the range of options for local faculties. At the crucial points of contact among teachers, students, and instructional resources, variety continues to rule.

JACK W. MILLER is Professor of Education and Director, Advanced Graduate Programs for Curriculum Leadership Personnel, George Peabody College for Teachers, Nashville, Tennessee. EDWARD V. JOHNSON is Doctoral Research Assistant, Advanced Graduate Programs for Curriculum Leadership Personnel, George Peabody College for Teachers, Nashville, Tennessee.

Perhaps the contemporary state of affairs is the result of some happy accident related to the frontier ethic—or perhaps it reflects a deeper spirit of independence that marks us all as distinctively human. Whatever the origin, we must accept the notion that content, sequence, and teacher-student interactions will continue to vary greatly in American social studies classrooms.

True, there *are* assembly lines and mass production aspects of the education enterprise. Label them textbooks, standardized tests, minimum standards for certification of teachers, accreditation regulations, state aid formulas, and HEW guidelines—if you wish. But under it all beats a free heart—the idiosyncratic mix of culture, heritage, needs, and desires held by millions of teachers, parents, and students.

Now we come to the essence of this concluding chapter. That is to provide sources—some pathways to ideas—for the use of classroom teachers and others engaged in social studies curriculum improvement. The books and pamphlets listed here are a varied lot. A dozen or more are the textbook variety. They represent their authors' and editors' distillation of the best advice to be found at a given time. Other sources are rich in new and unique ideas. Nearly all of them were chosen because they tell you how to do *something*. Somewhere in the listing you should find just the source needed for ideas, ways to plan how to carry out a program, or resources for effective teaching and evaluation.

We suggest that curriculum workers use the listing to begin a local, specialized collection. The nature of social studies curriculum revision projects varies, and so will the composition of the collection needed for individuals, committees, and others.

As to means, don't forget your librarians. Somewhere close—in your community and probably in your building—are qualified librarians who can help assemble the resource collection. Many of the books and pamphlets may be at hand already. Others will need to be ordered or borrowed on interlibrary loan. Just remember, a cooperative, trained librarian can locate and assemble more information quickly than can anyone on a typical curriculum improvement committee. Get a librarian on your team!

Getting Organized
for Curriculum Improvement

If significant and lasting changes are to be made in the quality of social studies instruction at the classroom level, key persons must engage in extensive preplanning of the project, as earlier chapters have pointed out. Large school systems in the United States employ special personnel—assistant superintendents, curriculum coordinators, or directors of instruction—to spearhead curriculum-building activity. In smaller school districts, however, responsibility for planning usually falls on individuals who are relatively unprepared and inexperienced in such work. As chairpersons or members of steering committees, they often need specific advice on the essential *how* of organizing a curriculum project.

Fortunately, several recent books carefully outline the human and mechanical aspects of curriculum study and revision. The five cited below should prove helpful to anyone charged with the coordination of a curriculum project.

Berman, Louise. *New Priorities in the Curriculum.* Columbus, Ohio: Charles E. Merrill, 1968. Argues for development of *process-oriented persons* as the critical goal of education. Following this line of reasoning, places the priority on teaching certain processes, rather than on traditional subjects. The human processes include perceiving, communicating, loving, knowing, decision making, patterning, creating, and valuing. Each is discussed in terms of importance, basic components, and application to teaching situations. A widely used text in the curriculum field.

English, Fenwick, and Kaufman, Roger. *Needs Assessment: A Focus for Curriculum Development.* Washington, D.C.: Association for Supervision and Curriculum Development, 1975. Guide for curriculum workers who want to know where to begin. Describes a step-by-step, logical process for a sequence of activities that can lead to a more "responsive" curriculum. Succinct.

Hass, Glenn. *Curriculum Planning: A New Approach.* Boston: Allyn & Bacon, 1977. Second edition of a highly successful textbook on curriculum planning. Can be a helpful guidebook for committee members (particularly those in leadership roles as chairpersons of task groups for sub-committees) on how to carry through the planning process with both involvement and coordination of several groups.

Oliver, Albert I. *Curriculum Improvement: A Guide to Problems, Principles, and Process.* New York: Harper & Row, 1977. Second edition that examines twelve basic planning problems—and encourages alternative approaches to solving them. Each chapter presents developmental activities that can help curriculum planning groups in making sound decisions. Emphasis on curriculum planning as a continuous, cooperative process.

Saylor, J. Galen, and Alexander, William M. *Planning Curriculum for Schools.* New York: Holt, Rinehart & Winston, 1974. Descriptions of various approaches to curriculum development, with a discussion of strengths and weaknesses. Has a strong chapter on evaluating curriculum plans and instruction. Valuable resource for curriculum planners who want to gain a good perspective of the process involved.

Tanner, Daniel, and Tanner, Laurel N. *Curriculum Development: Theory into Practice.* New York: Macmillan, 1975. Represents a well grounded, comprehensive statement on curriculum. Strongly supporting the writings of John Dewey, this text offers a basic history of curriculum development and advocates a high degree of teacher involvement in curriculum decision making. A valuable resource both for those who seek a thorough introduction to the field and for those who are already involved in it.

Background on Social Studies Planning

The preceding six references were general in nature. Social studies committees, of course, will also want some references aimed specifically at their field. Here are six—ranging from the 1969 NCSS Yearbook, dealing entirely with that topic, to summaries of research and research needs in the field.

Dunfee, Maxine. *Elementary School Social Studies: A Guide to Current Research.* Washington, D.C.: Association for Supervision and Curriculum Development, 1970. A survey of 351 studies dealing with goals, curriculum, child development, learning and inquiry, educational media, evaluation, and teacher education. Summaries are clustered under subheadings to help the reader locate particular concerns. Curriculum planners may find Part 2 (Social Studies Curriculum) and Part 6 (Evaluation in Social Studies) especially helpful.

Fraser, Dorothy McClure, editor. *Social Studies Curriculum Development: Prospects and Problems.* Washington, D.C.: National Council for the Social Studies, 1969. Comprehensive treatment of social studies curriculum reform, organized around critical decision-making areas. Noted authors contributed chapters that should aid local committees—as well as individual teachers—in identifying some of the critical decisions that must be

made. Has the great advantage of being focused entirely on the social studies, as well as being written under National Council auspices.

Haas, John D. *The Era of the New Social Studies.* Boulder, Colo.: Social Science Education Consortium, 1976. Mimeographed description of the origins, major actors, and accomplishments of the "new social studies." Could be a useful source document for curriculum committees interested in choosing materials. May help in avoiding repetition of errors others have made in initiation of new programs.

National Council for the Social Studies. *Social Studies Curriculum Guidelines: NCSS Position Statement.* Washington, D.C.: NCSS, 1971. Basic rationale for social studies education in the schools, with statements on the role of knowledge, abilities, valuing, and social participation in the curriculum. These are followed with 57 specific goals, organized under nine broad headings. Curriculum committees may find the "checklist for evaluating a social studies program" of particular value, since it presents a structure whereby local committee members can indicate (and then share) their level of agreement (strong, moderate, or slight) with each guideline statement.

Shaver, James P., and Larkins, A. Guy. "Research on Teaching Social Studies." In *Second Handbook of Research on Teaching,* pp. 1243–62. Edited by Robert M. W. Travers. Chicago: Rand McNally, 1973. While not a comprehensive review of research in social studies education, the chapter does provide an overview of basic findings and issues. Contains references to 86 studies, which deal with defining social studies, identifying needed research, and describing common research methodology and design. Note of interest—pp. 784–85 of the SHRT chapter on teaching of affective responses also contain a section on social studies.

Skretting, J. R., and Sundeen, James E. "Social Studies Education." In *Encyclopedia of Educational Research,* pp. 1231–41. Edited by Robert L. Ebel. Toronto: Collier Macmillan, 1969. Reports on significant research (conducted mainly in the 1960s) related to teaching of social studies at the elementary and secondary levels. Included are sections on content sources, curriculum organization, materials, evaluation, and teacher education. Curriculum committee members also may wish to use the EER as a source for accumulated research findings on any one of several dozen issues that may arise. Fortunately, a well-indexed reference work.

Formative and Summative Evaluation

Educators frequently are criticized for plunging into new programs without assessing where they are—or giving too much analytical thought to where they may be headed. Local needs and preferences may vary, but here are some references on how to set up and run formative (ongoing, modification as the data come in) and summative (classical pretest-posttest) evaluation systems. To carry through on most of them requires early involvement of technical help. Larger school districts have research departments and other sources of personnel with research design and assessment skills. Smaller districts may find help at a local college or university. Frequently, major universities with graduate programs in social studies education or curriculum design may have faculty-student teams that are interested in field-work sites. Two or three doctoral interns can provide a valuable boost to the efforts of a local group.

Whatever the human resources in *your* locality, here are some background references on the subject of program evaluation.

Bloom, Benjamin S.; Hastings, J. T.; and Madus, G. F.; editors. *Handbook on Formative and Summative Evaluation of Student Learning.* New York: McGraw-Hill, 1971. As the title indicates, an extensive collection of articles on "what is" and "how to." As curriculum committees begin to consider setting up an evaluative system for determining whether their new program is achieving its stated goals and meeting the needs of students, references such as this can be tremendously valuable. The public, which after all pays for the schools and sends the children who constitute the clientele, makes increasing and justified demands for accountability. This is particularly true of innovative curricula in sensitive, "soft" areas such as social studies.

Buros, Oscar K. *Social Studies Tests and Reviews.* Highland Park, N.J.: Gryphon Press, 1975. Combines the social studies sections of the *Mental Measurements Yearbooks* and *Tests in Print II.* Includes test descriptions, critiques, bibliographies for individual tests, and a directory of publishers. The tests are indexed in several ways and, as a bonus, there is a classified index to tests in other subject areas. A valuable source for anyone who needs to know the strengths and weaknesses of tests being used to assess social studies learning.

Fair, Jean, editor. *National Assessment and Social Studies Education: A Review of Assessments in Citizenship and Social Studies* (National Council for the Social Studies). Washington, D.C.: U.S. Government Printing Of-

policy bodies realize that schooling does not mean standard students, teachers, programs, and learning, they do tend to expect some kind of clear statement of broad goals or outcomes.

We have been concerned with the number of curriculum committees that waste time either in writing long lists of goals "from scratch"—or who plagiarize a set of meaningless goals from elsewhere. What seems needed, in many situations, is an intermediate approach. This likely should involve discussions among local groups—including parents and students—and a structured selection or adaptation of goal statements. Some of the references which follow provide background and rationale for inclusion of higher thought processes and affective elements in the program (such as Taxonomies). Other references provide long lists of "correctly worded" behavioral objectives that can be adapted rather easily to express local priorities.

Bloom, Benjamin S., editor. *Taxonomy of Educational Objectives: Handbook I: Cognitive Domain.* New York: Longmans, Green, 1956. *The* standard reference for classifying educational objectives in the cognitive area. Also useful to curriculum committees in classification of test questions or activities recommended in published sources, or forwarded by local sub-committees. The *Taxonomy* presents a rationale, full and detailed outline of its various levels, and exercises so that the reader-user can practice classification of objectives and compare the results with that of experts who originally designed and validated the *Taxonomy.*

Flanagan, John C.; Shanner, William M.; and Mager, Robert F. *Social Studies Behavioral Objectives: A Guide to Individualizing Learning.* Sunny-vale, Cal.: Westinghouse Learning Press, 1971. Curriculum committees struggling to write specific objectives for social studies classes at the primary, intermediate, and secondary school levels may find this a useful compilation. (Those opposed to such a notion may find it a useful example of what they do not like!) Several hundred objectives are included to cover all of the traditional social science discipline fields.

Kapfer, Miriam B., compiler. *Behavioral Objectives in Curriculum Development.* Englewood Cliffs, N.J.: Educational Technology Publications, 1971. A wide selection of significant readings on behavioral objectives as an educational tool. Both theoretical and practical aspects are included in this well organized collection. Curriculum planning groups will appreciate Part IV, on behavioral objectives and the curriculum developer, and Part VI, on behavioral objectives and the curriculum evaluator. A concluding section organizes a "debate-in-print" with articles from opposing viewpoints.

Krathwohl, David R.; Bloom, Benjamin S.; and Masia, B. B. *Taxonomy of Educational Objectives: Handbook II: Affective Domain.* New York: David McKay, 1964. This companion to *Handbook I: Cognitive Domain* is coming into increasing acceptance. Many social studies curriculum groups will want to key some of the goals and activities suggested for each grade level to the cognitive and affective domains. Alternatives to this handbook, of course, include the Kohlberg and values clarification materials now on the market.

Objectives for Instructional Programs. Huntington Beach, Cal.: Insgroup, 1977. A multimedia package for training school personnel, including curriculum committees, in identifying and specifying objectives. If curriculum committees are under a mandate to specify overall goals and specific objectives—possibly listed in behavioral or at least measurable terms—they may want to invest in this or a similar package. Can involve up to 40 hours of self-based or small-group instruction. Includes charts, filmstrips, workbooks, and needs assessment materials.

Tri-County Goal Development Project. *Course Goals for K-12 Social Science: Anthropology, Economics, Geography, History, Political Science, Psychology, and Sociology.* Portland, Oregon: Northwest Regional Educational Laboratory, 1976. Compilation of more than 5,000 goals statements developed by 55 cooperative school districts in the Portland area. Each goal is coded to taxonomies of knowledge, process, and values—based somewhat on the work of Bloom, Gagné, Piaget, Krathwohl, Walbesser, Tyler, and Mager. The goals also are coded to indicate the grade level at which they might be placed. There are special sections on value clarification, choices, process of inquiry, and problem solving. Curriculum committees may find this an extremely useful resource in identifying local goals, and in writing them up in proper form—if such a step becomes a part of the curriculum development process. Even if it does not, the listing of goals and rationale behind them should be informative and useful.

Determination of Scope and Sequence

Expanding knowledge, the pressures of citizenship at age eighteen, and national political crises seem to have led many school districts to both update and expand the scope of their social studies programs. While European and American history still domi-

nate a majority of programs, the social sciences are receiving increased attention.

Unfortunately, some curriculum guides have incorporated goals statements that seem to imply a broad, humanistic, and contemporary orientation, but then fail to specify how, when, or by whom these things were to be done. Such developments are not surprising, however. How could many local curriculum committees hope to have access to expert representation from fields such as cultural anthropology, sociology, social psychology—or even political science and economics?

Nor have local committees had access to plainly written but authoritative material on these topics—material that could be adapted to elementary and high school programs.

Fortunately, the situation has improved. The 1960s witnessed a boom in production of content-outlines, material on new processes of inquiry and problem resolution, and applications for different kinds of learners. The sampling below should be supplemented by the many other references in later sections of this chapter.

Association of American Geographers and the American Sociological Association. *Experiences in Inquiry: HSGP and SRSS.* Boston: Allyn & Bacon, 1974. Uses the High School Geography Project and Sociological Resources for the Social Studies materials as a springboard for curriculum and teaching activity descriptions. Local committees may find it a useful source of ideas for ways to use these and other "new social studies" project materials.

Bacon, Phillip, editor. *Focus on Geography: Key Concepts and Teaching Strategies.* Washington, D.C.: National Council for the Social Studies, 1970. An affirmation of the partnership of geography and human behavior. Part One presents concepts and techniques in geography that are understandable even to the "non-geographer." Part Two deals with the search for classroom applications that will be truly relevant for students at all levels.

Beyer, Barry K., and Penna, Anthony N., editors. *Concepts in the Social Studies.* Washington, D.C.: National Council for the Social Studies, 1973. Curriculum committees concerned with developing a program around basic concepts, generalizations, and understandings likely will find this bulletin extremely useful. Expert authors discuss the difference between isolated facts of knowledge and basic concepts. They also offer many useful suggestions for how to teach concepts in the classroom.

Gross, Richard E., and Muessig, Raymond H., editors. *Problem-Centered Social Studies Instruction: Approaches to Reflective Teaching.* Washington, D.C.: National Council for the Social Studies, 1971. Series of articles on the problem resolution method of social studies teaching. Included are discussions of current trends in problem solving and a listing of teaching resources for the problems approach.

Herbert, Louis J., and Murphy, William, editors. *Structure in the Social Studies.* Washington, D.C.: National Council for the Social Studies, 1968. Presents a broad sampling of meanings given to the term "structure" and deals with the implications of those meanings for the social studies curriculum. Some of the approaches examined involve curricula based on human activities, inquiry skills, and values systems.

Millar, Jayne C. *Focusing on Global Poverty and Development: A Resource Book for Educators.* Washington,

D.C.: Overseas Development Council, 1974. Considered one of the best resources on ways to build in a world view for the social studies curriculum. Section I contains brief essays which suggest ways to provide a global perspective in courses such as United States history, economics, anthropology, world history, etc. The second section presents essays on topics such as population, hunger, and affluence in an interdependent world; modernization and change; and the global crisis in jobs. Part III includes maps, charts, case studies, a selective film guide, and a glossary of terms.

Morrissett, Irving, and Stevens, W. Williams, Jr., editors. *Social Science in the Schools: A Search for Rationale.* New York: Holt, Rinehart & Winston, 1971. Based on a social studies conference held at Purdue University. Among the important themes are synthesis of the social sciences and cooperative/competitive relationships among the social sciences. Much of the content has implications for teacher education, especially the round table discussion in Chapter 17, and would be helpful in planning in-service programs.

Opposing Viewpoints Series. Minneapolis: Green Haven Press. Green Haven Press, for a number of years, has specialized in production of contemporary issues materials. Curriculum committees may want to examine some of these booklets, games, photo study sets, cassettes, and other materials, both as possibilities for the program that is finally developed and for ideas on contemporary elements which should be built into the scope and sequence of a new curriculum. These and similar materials should prove especially helpful for committees whose own background and orientation have been excessively focused on the traditional history-geography-government pattern of curriculum.

Remy, Richard C.; Nathan, James A.; Becker, James M.; and Torney, Judith V. *International Learning and International Education in a Global Age.* Washington, D.C.: National Council for the Social Studies, 1975. Provides information and ideas about international study with the goal of improving instruction in this area. After a review of the current state of social science knowledge on the topic, the authors present alternative ways of viewing the world and then discuss the design of world studies programs in regard to attendant problems and issues.

The Social Studies and the Social Sciences. New York: Harcourt, Brace & World, 1962. Product of a four-year effort by the American Council of Learned Societies and the National Council for the Social Studies. Well organized statements of content and objectives are made by scholars in history, geography, political science, economics, cultural anthropology, sociology, and psychology. There are also statements on the area studies of Asia and Eastern Europe. A committee of the National Council for the Social Studies concluded the volume with a discussion of the overall objectives of secondary school social studies.

Toffler, Alvin, editor. *Learning for Tomorrow: The Role of the Future in Education.* New York: Vintage Books, 1974. As the title suggests, this book is oriented toward ways of introducing futurism—or the choices that young people now in school will later face—in the social studies classroom. It also may help the committee members broaden their own horizons and gain a new perspective on the role and focus of the local curriculum.

Turner, Mary Jane, and Haley, Frances. *Utilization of New Social Studies Curriculum Programs.* Boulder, Colo.: Social Science Education Consortium, 1975. Mimeographed report of a survey of social studies teachers in four states. Focuses on the use of nine "new social studies" curriculum packages available in the early 1970s.

Curriculum Building Aids

Curriculum revision projects often are focused either on the elementary or the secondary school level. In some cases, a massive K-12 revision may be underway, but the decision is made to subdivide the group for the sake of efficiency and convenience. In either instance, there likely will be a need for source materials which are devoted specifically to elementary or to high school social studies—and the selections below are divided accordingly.

It should be noted that the two lists include several volumes which are excellent teaching aids, in addition to offering direction to curriculum workers. Obviously, these books should be purchased and used for both purposes. Separate listings of references which are primarily teaching aids have been placed near the end of this chapter.

Elementary Focus

Ahern, John F., and Lucas, Nanci D. *Ideas: A Handbook for Elementary Social Studies.* New York: Harper & Row, 1975. A true handbook—not a textbook—that presents a multitude of workable ideas for a humanistic approach to teaching social studies. Among the areas of interest are learning centers, role-playing, team teaching, use of local resources, and student-made media. Also, a section on teacher-created units features ten ways to introduce, forty-six ways to develop, and eight ways to conclude a unit.

Crowder, William W. *Persistent-Problems Approach to Elementary Social Studies.* Itasca, Ill.: F. E. Peacock, 1973. Suggests seven persistent individual and societal problems as a curriculum base for elementary school social studies. A thorough explanation of the approach is followed by suggestions for implementation, featuring an engaging chapter on using maps and globes. Strong emphasis on self-awareness as a goal for young people.

Ellis, Arthur K. *Teaching and Learning Elementary Social Studies.* Boston: Allyn & Bacon, 1977. Good, standard reference text for elementary social studies. Contains the usual chapters on the background and rationale for elementary social studies, trends in curriculum, and ideas on teaching strategies and materials.

Hanna, Lavone A.; Potter, Gladys L.; and Reynolds, Robert W. *Dynamic Elementary Social Studies: Unit Teaching.* New York: Holt, Rinehart & Winston, 1973. Presents unit teaching as a process-oriented, child-centered approach. Affirming that the goal of social studies instruction is the development of responsible democratic citizens, the authors bring theory to reality through vignettes of actual classroom experiences. Added features in this third edition are chapters on "Dramatic Play, Role-Playing, and Simulation Games" and "Industrial Arts and Construction."

Jarolimek, John. *Social Studies in Elementary Education.* New York: Macmillan, 1977. Fifth edition of one of the most popular and commonly used curriculum and methods texts in the elementary school social studies field. Teachers tend to find the book clearly written and direct, with a reasonable marriage of theory and practical suggestions.

Jarolimek, John, and Walsh, Huber M., editors. *Readings for Social Studies in Elementary Education.* New York: Macmillan, 1974. Third and updated edition, arranged in seven broad areas. Features 63 significant articles, published mainly from 1969 to 1973. A noticeable development is that the literature has become, in general, more oriented toward human concerns. Use of a book of readings, such as this one, can save an enormous amount of sorting through specialized journals.

Lee, John R. *Teaching Social Studies in the Elementary School.* New York: Free Press, 1974. Teaching methods book appropriate for both preservice and inservice education. Written in a clear, conversational style, this volume is full of practical suggestions and sample lessons that can be put to immediate use. One of the book's strongest features is the author's presentation of entertaining yet relevant anecdotes.

Long, Barbara E. *The Journey to Myself: A Curriculum in Psychology for Middle Schools.* Austin, Texas: Steck-Vaughn, 1974. Curriculum committees sometimes need to examine alternatives to traditional patterns. This booklet, on how to introduce psychology for middle grade youngsters, may serve that purpose.

Michaelis, John U. *Social Studies for Children in a Democracy: Recent Trends and Developments.* Englewood Cliffs, N.J.: Prentice-Hall, 1976. Sixth edition of a highly respected text. Focuses on the task of combining new developments in social studies education with time-tested concepts from past experience. Features liberal use of helpful guidelines, charts, checklists that will help teachers improve instruction.

Michaelis, John U.; Grossman, Ruth H.; and Scott, Lloyd F. *New Designs for Elementary Curriculum and Instruction.* New York: McGraw-Hill, 1975. Provides a framework for analysis, development, and evaluation of the social studies curriculum at the elementary and middle school levels. Uses the taxonomies of cognitive and affective objectives in constructing evaluation instruments. The organization of this volume should make it useful to curriculum committees.

Oliner, Pearl M. *Teaching Elementary Social Studies: A Rational and Humanistic Approach.* New York: Harcourt, Brace, Jovanovich, 1977. Includes both theoretical concepts and practical planning ideas. The author deals with most aspects of social studies education, presenting specific teaching strategies and examples on current issues such as sexism and poverty.

Ord, John E. *Elementary School Social Studies for Today's Children.* New York: Harper & Row, 1972. Identifies major approaches, trends, and developments in social studies education. Two helpful features are the chapter on evaluation (stressing the use of behavioral objectives as a guide) and an appendix containing sample teaching units.

Overly, Norman V., and Kimpston, Richard D., editors. *Global Studies: Problems and Promises for Elementary Teachers.* Washington, D.C.: Association for Supervision and Curriculum Development, 1976. A challenging discussion of an important educational issue. The various selections present rationale, content, and materials for teaching about world problems at the elementary level.

Preston, Ralph C., and Herman, Wayne L., Jr. *Teaching Social Studies in the Elementary School.* New York: Holt, Rinehart & Winston, 1974. A

fourth edition expanded from thirteen to twenty-two chapters. This volume covers a lot of territory, including a strong section on children as learners. Teachers will be especially interested in the miscellany of down-to-earth teaching tasks discussed in the final section, as well as the "boxes" of teaching tips sprinkled throughout the text.

Skeel, Dorothy J. *The Challenge of Teaching Social Studies in the Elementary School.* Pacific Palisades, Cal.: Goodyear, 1970. Presents a variety of strategies for teaching social studies and provides practical applications to classroom settings. Chapter 2 has useful information on selected social studies projects at the local, state, and national levels. Not designed strictly for teachers, this text should also appeal to supervisors and curriculum planners.

Thomas, R. Murray, and Brubaker, Dale L. *Curriculum Patterns in Elementary Social Studies.* Belmont, Cal.: Wadsworth Publishing, 1971. Describes a variety of social studies programs and analyzes them in terms of theoretical foundations and classroom application. A specific set of criteria is used for a comparative discussion of five comprehensive programs, including those of Hanna and Taba, and five partial programs. This book should interest curriculum workers who want to know about available alternatives.

Welton, David A., and Mallan, John T. *Children and Their World: Teaching Elementary Social Studies.* Chicago: Rand McNally, 1977. Contemporary curriculum and methods text focused on elementary school social studies. Good background reading for curriculum committee members who have not worked in the social studies area or who have specialized in junior or senior high teaching. Chapters on what should be taught, means of organizing the program, values education, and numerous practical classroom strategies. An instructor's manual also is available.

Secondary Focus

Cartwright, William H., and Watson, Richard L., editors. *Reinterpretation of American History and Culture.* Washington, D.C.: National Council for the Social Studies, 1973. Twenty-six essays provide an update and rationale for maintaining history in the curriculum. If a new social studies curriculum is to include extensive coverage of multi-culture heritage, women's roles, consumerism, values, sociology, and other topics, the present emphasis on history is likely to diminish. While this may be appropriate in some situations, the revision needs to be done thoughtfully and deliberately, so that committees are ready to defend actions to themselves and to their constituencies.

Ehman, Lee; Mehlinger, Howard; and Patrick, John. *Toward Effective Instruction in Secondary Social Studies.* Boston: Houghton Mifflin, 1974. Competency-oriented treatment of social studies teaching, with emphasis on how to *think* about the instructional process. Deals with four teacher roles—curriculum planner, instructor, evaluator, and professional educator—and makes liberal use of illustrative examples from social studies projects and other sources. A feature that adds interest is the use of dialogues with characters representing various viewpoints on educational practices. Committees also may find the discussion of norm and criterion referenced evaluation in social studies quite useful.

Gardner, William E., and Johnson, Fred A., editors. *Social Studies in the*

Secondary School: A Book of Readings. Boston: Allyn & Bacon, 1970. Provides an overview of problems and issues in high school social studies education. Includes useful discussions of promising methods and materials available in the early 1970s. This volume would be a good starting place for background reading in preparation for a curriculum revision project.

Kownslar, Allan O., editor. *Teaching American History: The Quest for Relevancy.* Washington, D.C.: National Council for the Social Studies, 1974. Technically speaking, this yearbook is not a curriculum outline or guide. Rather, it focuses on specific, contemporary lessons that can be presented in American history classes at the high school level. Selected chapters, however, could be very useful for curriculum committee members who teach at the elementary school level, for administrators and the secondary school teachers who may not be aware of some of the newer trends in American history teaching, and for citizen committee members who need something to replace their own high school recollections.

Newmann, Fred M. *Education for Citizen Action: Challenge for Secondary Curriculum.* Berkeley: McCutchan, 1975. Interesting "think piece" book on designing high school social studies programs with the intent of exerting influence on public affairs. Using this social action approach, the author goes on to outline skills and competencies that a secondary school social studies program might develop. Also discusses the anticipated local barrier to implementation of such a program.

Phillips, Richard C. *Teaching for Thinking in High School Social Studies.* Menlo Park, Cal.: Addison-Wesley, 1974. A methods text based on the view that *the* primary goal in social studies instruction should be to teach students how to think effectively about critical social problems. Included are chapters on value analysis, developing curriculum, and evaluation. Sample classroom dialogue is used to illustrate many of the ideas and concepts presented.

Pratt, Robert B. *Perspectives: A Social Studies Handbook for Secondary Teachers, 7–12.* Des Moines: Iowa State Department of Public Instruction, 1974. Provides information to assist teachers in implementing curriculum innovations and evaluating their social studies programs. Important features of this thoughtfully organized volume are a ten-step revision process and a helpful resource guide on social studies projects, simulation games, and publications (mostly from the 1970s).

Sistrunk, Walter E., and Maxson, Robert C. *A Practical Approach to Secondary Social Studies.* Dubuque, Iowa: William C. Brown, 1972. A "cookbook" approach for teachers who want the best of two worlds—proven old practices and promising new practices. Essentially a methods text, this volume deals with everyday concerns of teachers, including planning, selection of materials, and grading. Nearly half of the book is devoted to examples of teaching units and courses of study both for middle schools and high schools.

Stephens, Lester D. *Probing the Past: A Guide to the Study and Teaching of History.* Boston: Allyn & Bacon, 1974. Curriculum committee members should gain some valuable ideas on practical applications to the inquiry approach—as well as ways to interrelate history and the social sciences. After presenting a rationale and outline in part one, the author illustrates these ideas in a second section of the book.

Wager, W. Warren. *Books in World History: A Guide for Teachers and Students.* Bloomington: Indiana University Press, 1973. An annotated bibliography of materials for teaching world history. Ten ways to structure world history courses are suggested, and broad fields are explored, including Middle Eastern history, African history, and Latin American history.

Wesley, Edgar B., and Wronski, Stanley P. *Teaching Secondary Social Studies in a World Society.* Lexington, Mass.: D. C. Heath, 1973. Sixth edition of a classic methods text. Based on a world view of social studies, the book contains much useful information for curriculum decision making. Also offers many suggestions for classroom use of materials and communication techniques. Numerous charts, illustrations, and examples bring out most of the central concepts quite clearly.

Wood, Leslie A. *Contemporary Strategies in Teaching Social Studies, Junior and Senior High School: Sampler, Authoritative Commentary and Bibliography, and Annotated Bibliography.* Northfield, Ill.: Cooperative Educational Research Laboratory (also published by U.S. Government Printing Office), 1969. Provides a useful cataloging and brief explanation for more than 50 teaching strategies that have proven effective with adolescent learners. Individual teachers, a curriculum committee, or others can use the listing to (1) determine how often a particular strategy is currently utilized, and (2) indicate how high a priority should be placed on that particular strategy in the local situation. The booklet also has an excellent annotated bibliography and commentary related to research and school system trials of teaching strategies and materials from the late 1950s through the 1960s.

Recent Social Studies Curriculum Guides

The decentralized pattern of education in the United States has afforded an unusual opportunity to develop a variety of instructional programs. Every year dozens of school systems release the printed outlines which summarize the new social studies curricula for their schools. Certainly, a group of educators charged with the responsibility of developing a new curriculum guide for their school system will want to examine the work of others for information and inspiration. Often the most immediate source for such materials is a curriculum library maintained by a local school district, college, or university. If such a source is not at hand, it may well be fruitful for the local group to purchase a number of recent curriculum bulletins and courses of study from other school districts.

Social Education, the journal of the National Council for the Social Studies, carries a considerable amount of material on new programs. These include discussions of exciting, overall plans and reviews of films, text series, trade books, and teaching approaches. In the mid-1970s, a Curriculum Information Network (CIN) was formed. Among other services, this organization regularly publishes summaries on reactions of individuals who have used some of the new program material in the field.

Persons able to attend an annual meeting of the NCSS, usually held about Thanksgiving time, can examine local school system materials on display. They also can talk with the dozens of publishers who exhibit maps, films, books, and other instructional materials at the conference.

Another annual listing of curriculum guides is contained in a publication of the Association for Supervision and Curriculum Development. Curriculum guides in social studies, as well as other areas, are displayed at the association's annual conference in March. The association usually publishes a listing of the guides, entitled *Curriculum Materials—1978* (or some variation). This listing would be a valuable source for ordering samples for the local collection.

A rich resource that should not be overlooked is ERIC (Educational Resources Information Center), an easy-to-use retrieval system located in the libraries of many colleges and universities. One "branch" of the system is *Resources in Education*, a monthly publication that provides abstracts of valuable unpublished articles, bulletins, etc.—all classified by subject area, author, institution, and accession number. A separate volume, the *Thesaurus of ERIC Descriptors*, lists the terms under which ERIC documents are classified, two examples being "social studies" and "social studies units."

Also helpful are the annual and semi-annual indexes. The 1976 January-June index, for instance, listed 66 documents under "social studies." These included several on religion in education, values education, and specific foreign cultures. There were 31 documents named under "social studies units," with topics such as career education, environmental problems, minorities, and food shortages in the world. Ultimately, the investigator is led to microfiche—not "fish" but "feesh"—that can be placed on a special viewer for reading. With this you can read the entire document and, if you wish, have copies made inexpensively. Another option is to order a computer search for ERIC holdings on specific topics of interest.

Because of the availability of

NCSS, ASCD, ERIC, and other listings—and the rapid obsolescence of such items—no attempt is made here to identify specific names or sources of outstanding local school system curriculum guides in the social studies. Your committee will want to build and index a current collection, geared to local needs.

Instructional Aids for Teachers

Social studies teachers are noted for their interest in obtaining new materials for professional and classroom use. This intense interest seems quite natural, for an effective social studies program ought to be concerned with an intellectual, social, and physical world which is changing constantly.

Several sample bibliographies are presented in this section. They include a general listing on teaching ideas, a selection of booklists for various grade levels, compilations of free and inexpensive materials, media guides, and activity sourcebooks.

General Resources

Berger, Evelyn, and Winters, Bonnie A. *Social Studies in the Open Classroom: A Practical Guide.* New York: Teachers College Press, 1973. Useful reference for coming up-to-date on the open classroom concept. Also a recommended source for teachers in the process of implementing a new, pupil-oriented social studies curriculum.

Chase, W. Linwood, and John, Martha Tyler. *A Guide for the Elementary Social Studies Teacher.* Boston: Allyn & Bacon, 1972. Presents a multitude of practical suggestions for teachers, with a minimum of theorizing and philosophizing. Has a great deal of new material and a something-for-everyone appeal, supplementing the text with numerous charts and ex-

amples. Teachers may especially appreciate the section on improving services to the individual child.

Hunkins, Francis P., and Spears, Patricia F. *Social Studies for the Evolving Individual.* Washington, D.C.: Association for Supervision and Curriculum Development, 1973. Brief but meaningful look at some viewpoints on goals, content, and methods for social education in a changing society. This little volume provides an overview for educators at all levels.

Kenworthy, Leonard S. *Social Studies for the Seventies.* Lexington, Mass.: Xerox College Publishing, 1973. An updated teachers' guidebook that includes new sections on ecology, conflict resolution, war and peace, and Africa. Outlines and evaluates new programs, gives many examples of modern learning strategies, and discusses new materials. Numerous bibliographies throughout the text allow the reader to pursue favorite topics in depth.

Martorella, Peter H. *Concept Learning in the Social Studies.* Scranton, Pa.: Intext Educational Publishers, 1971. Presents several models for a curriculum based on concept learning, along with some elucidating concept-learning exercises. Parts One, Three, and Four seem well suited for use in workshop-type sessions for teachers. Part Three deals more with theoretical and research-oriented concerns.

Massialas, Byron G.; Sprague, Nancy F.; and Hurst, Joseph B. *Social Issues Through Inquiry: Coping in an Age of Crisis.* Englewood Cliffs, N.J.: Prentice-Hall, 1975. Presents a model program of instruction based on a seven-year research project. The inquiry method of learning is applied to a social-issues approach, using sample classroom dialogue to bring theory to a down-to-earth level. The concluding chapter makes suggestions for positive action to improve the social studies curriculum.

Morse, Horace T., and McCune, George H. Revised by Lester E. Brown and Ellen Cook. *Selected Items for the Testing of Study Skills and Critical Thinking.* Washington, D.C.: National Council for the Social Studies, 1971. Presents the rationale and outline of elements of critical thinking and study skills—and how these relate to the immediate classroom situation. Contains practical suggestions for teachers, test ideas, and sample materials for classroom use. Could be a valuable source of ideas for social studies objectives—or a reference for teachers who wish to move beyond the fact and knowledge level in classroom assessments.

Muessig, Raymond H., editor. *Controversial Issues in the Social Studies: A Contemporary Perspective.* Washington, D.C.: National Council for the Social Studies, 1975. Curriculum committees likely will have to confront the need for a policy statement on handling controversial issues in the social studies, unless the "revolutionary new program" is to be confined to the dead, the old, the dull, and the nonrelevant. Once having made a commitment to provide students with opportunities to consider value choices and controversial, contemporary issues in their community and the nation, the committee likely will be confronted with any number of difficult choices. This yearbook discusses a number of mid-1970s issues and presents viewpoints handling them both in development of curriculum guides and in classroom operations.

Preston, Ralph C., editor. *A New Look at Reading in the Social Studies.* Newark: International Reading Association, 1969. Presents research data outlining the problems that many students experience with social studies reading material. Curriculum committees should be sensitive to reading and concept-loading problems in typical social studies material, so that a revised curriculum can be used with the diverse groups of students found in most major school systems. Otherwise, the print-oriented members of curriculum study committees are likely to produce a program appropriate only for the upper one-fourth or one-half of the student population.

Public Affairs Pamphlets Social Issues. New York: Public Affairs Committee. A series of useful and current pamphlets on various social issues, this selection constitutes another resource for curriculum committees seeking to obtain ideas for possible perspectives and content of a new program.

Roselle, Daniel. *A Parent's Guide to the Social Studies.* Washington, D.C.: National Council for the Social Studies, 1974. Not a guide for new program proposals from curriculum committees, but may be extremely useful for orientation of citizens' groups concerned with the present program and apprehensive about change. Contents include answers to such questions as "What are the social studies?"; "How are the social studies taught?"; "Why do social studies educators say that knowing information is not enough?"; "How can parents help their children in the social studies?" Available in bulk from the National Council.

Ruchlis, Hy, and Sharefkin, Belle. *Reality-Centered Learning.* New York: Citation Press, 1975. Presents a rationale for classroom studies focused on issues that students consider "real." Advocates lessons using inquiry, problem solving, interdisciplinary investigations, and active involvement of the class group. Also provides suggestions for reality-centered lessons on many different levels and different subject areas, including social studies topics.

Ubbelohde, Carl, and Fraenkel, Jack R., editors. *Values of the American Heritage: Challenges, Case Studies, and Teaching Strategies.* Washington, D.C.: National Council for the Social Studies, 1976. A selective examination, in "case study" form, of concepts and ideas on the development of the United States as an independent nation. Part One concerns the promises of the Declaration of Independence, while Part Two focuses on the teaching of values and features many illustrative examples.

Xerox Unit Books. Columbus, Ohio: Xerox Education Publications. Several series of inexpensive paper bulletins on such contemporary issues as ethnic and urban studies, ecology and the environment, values and decisions, area studies, and public issues. Though booklets are intended for middle and secondary school students, some topics can provide valuable insights and information to a curriculum committee as it establishes overall objectives and begins to lay out the scope and sequence of a modern program.

Booklists and Reading Guides

Brown, Ralph A., and Brown, Marian R. *American History Book List for High Schools: A Selection for Supplementary Reading.* Washington, D.C.: National Council for the Social Studies, 1969. A guide intended for the busy history teacher who wants to know, quickly and easily, what is available for supplemental reading. Each book in this extensive list is classified according to nature of content, reading level, and type of binding.

Haley, Frances, and McCormick, Regina. *Directory of Social Studies/Social Science Service Organizations.* Boulder, Colo.: Social Science Education Consortium, 1976. Useful compilation of more than 100 social studies and social science education service organizations. Provides information on types of services offered, target grade levels, subject areas, goals, current projects, and publications of each organization.

McLendon, Jonathon C., editor. *Guide to Reading for Social Studies Teachers.* Washington, D.C.: National Council for the Social Studies, 1973. Lists over 1300 publications for social studies teachers. Written by recognized authorities in each specific area of concern, chapters are organized into sections on the social sciences; societal problems and issues; curriculum, methods, and media; and perspectives on human development.

President's Committee on Consumer Interests. *Suggested Guidelines for Consumer Education: Kindergarten through Twelfth Grade.* Washington, D.C.: Superintendent of Documents, U.S. Government Printing Office, 1970. Succinct guidelines for incorporating consumer education into the K-12 social studies curriculum. Committee members also should check with the Government Printing Office for a revised edition of these guidelines and/or other materials to use in setting goals and organizing a consumer education strand or specific units for different grade levels.

Social Studies Curriculum Materials Data Book. Boulder, Colo.: Social Science Education Consortium, 1970s (current). A "blockbuster" reference source that includes analyses of over 350 social studies materials, including projects, textbooks, supplementary materials, games and simulations, and teacher resources. Comes in loose-

leaf notebook form so that annual supplements can be added. An extremely valuable reference resource for curriculum committees and subcommittees that are choosing materials.
Social Studies in the Intermediate Grades: An Annotated Bibliography. Washington, D.C.: National Education Association, 1975. A valuable source for locating teaching materials for grades 4-8.

World Civilization Booklist Committee of NCSS, Morris Gall and Arthur E. Soderlind, Chairpersons. *World Civilization Booklist: Supplementary Reading for Secondary Schools.* Washington, D.C.: National Council for the Social Studies, 1968. Annotated list of more than 1200 publications on world history, both fiction and nonfiction. Books are listed in Part One according to time periods, topics, and geographic areas, while annotations in Part Two are given by author's last name. A special feature is the coding of entries to signify appropriate reading level.

**Lists of Free
and Inexpensive Materials**

American Problems. Englewood Cliffs, N.J.: Prentice-Hall (current dating). An example of a new and continuing trend in the social studies: quick publication of background facts, points of view, and study guide materials for examination of critical choices facing citizens in the United States. Curriculum committees likely will want to collect materials from several such sources in order to become current and to identify new approaches in organizing and delivering social studies instructional experiences.

Consumers Union Education Materials. Orangeburg, New York: Consumers Union, mid-1970s. The Consumers Union, which publishes the well known *Consumer Reports* and *Annual Buyers Guide*, also has collaborated in the preparation of key study and other materials for school use. As a first step, the curriculum committee might write to Consumers Union, stating the committee's interests and needs. This should bring a response with a list of materials available and, perhaps, some suggestions for contact persons who could help the committee in its work.

Educators Guide to Free Social Studies Materials: A Multi-Media Guide. 17th edition. Randolph, Wisc.: Educators Progress Service, 1977. A massive, annually revised listing of films, exhibits, slides, audio tapes, charts, magazines, transcriptions, filmstrips, videotapes, scripts, posters, and other materials available on a free or free-loan basis. Readers who are unfamiliar with this source undoubtedly will find copies somewhere in the system, perhaps in every school library. A new edition appears early each fall, with automatic mailing and billing to those who wish it.

Foreign Policy Association Publications. New York: FPA. Includes the *Headline Series, Great Decisions*, and many specialized booklets on world problems and crises. Curriculum committee members may wish to review some of these materials for ideas or topics to be included in a proposed program. Also is a source to be listed in bibliographies that accompany new curriculum guides.

Free and Inexpensive Learning Materials. 19th edition. Nashville, Tenn: Office of Educational Services, George Peabody College for Teachers, 1978. An annotated listing of several thousand free or inexpensive educational materials. Each piece of material has been carefully screened for school use. Annotations contain full information on availability and prices, as well as the address of the distributor. The book is kept up-to-date through biennial revisions (1980, 1982, etc.). Teachers at all grade levels will find an abundance of charts, posters, pictures, multimedia kits, booklets, pamphlets, and other materials to enrich their social studies instruction. Since the guide also covers other curriculum fields, topics of interest can be located through use of the table of contents or the comprehensive index.

Population Reference Bureau Publications. Washington, D.C.: Population Reference Bureau (current dating). Curriculum committees wishing to include contemporary information on world population trends and problems should examine low-cost materials available from the PRB: pamphlets, classroom study guide materials, books, transparency masters, and other useful teaching/curriculum aids.

Selected U.S. Government Publications. Washington, D.C.: Superintendent of Documents, U.S. Government Printing Office. Through this free monthly booklet, curriculum committee members and teachers can keep abreast of the enormous volume of low-cost, generally high quality topical materials published by the Government Printing Office. These publications may be purchased over the counter in 15-20 distribution centers or may be ordered by mail from Washington.

Social Education. Washington, D.C.: National Council for the Social Studies. 7 issues per year. For years, *Social Education* has carried sections on instructional media; new books in the field; various editorials, articles, research reports; and commentary on curriculum issues affecting the social studies field. Curriculum committees would do well to systematically ex-

amine back issues of *Social Education* for both background "think" pieces and for specific ideas in structuring or implementing curriculum plans. Another source of information, of course, are the numerous advertisements which appear each month.

Spurgin, John H., and Smith, Gary R. *Global Dimensions in the New Social Studies.* Boulder, Colo.: ERIC Clearinghouse for Social Studies/Social Science Education, 1973. Contains reviews of several of the "new social studies" projects from the standpoint of their global, rather than national, emphasis. Curriculum committees can use these reviews for assessing program elements that they may wish to adopt locally, as well as for a source for ideas in locally-created curricula.

Media Guides

Kuhns, William. *Themes Two.* Dayton, Ohio: Pflaum/Standard, 1974. A media resource book describing 100 short films for enrichment of instruction in secondary schools. Each description contains a synopsis, and all titles are cross-referenced in a thematic index.

Rufsbold, Margaret, and Guss, Carolyn. *Guides to Educational Media: Films, Filmstrips, Kinescopes, Phonodiscs, Phonotapes, Programmed Instruction Materials, Slides, Transparencies, and Videotapes.* Chicago: American Library Association, 1971. Lists and describes catalogs, services, professional organizations, journals, and periodicals that regularly provide information on educational media. Good resource to recommend to teachers and librarians (who may already have copies on hand) to list in a local curriculum guide.

Schrank, Jeffrey. *The Seed Catalog: A Guide to Teaching/Learning Materials.* Boston: Beacon Press, 1974. Oriented toward high school and adult learners. Listings include many provocative, creative, and controversial materials for social studies use.

Sprecher, Daniel. *Guide to Government-Loan Films* (16 mm); (with a separate section on filmstrips and slides). Alexandria, Va.: Serina Press, 1974. Extensive listing and descriptions of films, filmstrips, and slides produced by various government agencies. Organized by agency, but also includes a subject index and suggests grade levels.

In addition to general compilations of print and non-print materials, there are a number of specialized guides available. Here is a sampling:

● **Ackermann, Jean Marie.** *Films of a Changing World.* Washington, D.C.: Society of International Development, 1972.

● **Brown, Robert L.** *American Indian Teaching Materials: Films, Filmstrips, and Tapes.* Arcata, Cal.: California State University Bookstore, 1972.

● *Films and Filmstrips on Legal and Law-Related Subjects.* Chicago: Division of Communications, American Bar Association, 1973.

● **Goodman, Irwin R.** *Bibliography of Nonprint Instructional Materials on the American Indian.* Provo, Utah: Brigham Young University, Print Service, 1972.

● **Jablonsky, Adelaide.** *Media for Teaching Afro-American Studies.* New York: ERIC Clearinghouse on Urban Education, 1970.

● **Johnson, Harry A.** *Multimedia Materials for Afro-American Studies: A Curriculum Orientation and Annotated Bibliography of Resources.* New York: R.R. Bowker, 1971.

● **Lewis, Darrel R. et al.** *Educational Games and Simulations in Economics* (second edition). New York: Joint Council on Economic Education, 1974.

● **Nichols, Margaret S.** *Multicultural Bibliography for Pre-School Through Second Grade: In the Areas of Black, Spanish-Speaking, Asian-American, and Native American Cultures.* Stanford, Cal.: Multicultural Resources, 1972.

● **O'Connor, John E., and Jackson, Martin A.** *Teaching History with Film.* Washington, D.C.: American Historical Association.

● *Psychology Teachers' Resource Book.* Washington, D.C.: American Psychological Association, 1973.

Activity Sourcebooks

Canfield, Jack, and Wells, Harold C. *100 Ways to Enhance Self-Concept in the Classroom: A Handbook for Teachers and Parents.* Englewood Cliffs, N.J.: Prentice-Hall, 1976. Describes 100 proven strategies and techniques for enhancing self-concept. Activities are suitable for use with students of all ages and should be valuable to educators who are concerned about more humanistic approaches to teaching.

Charles, Cheryl, and Stadsklev, Ronald, editors. *Learning with Games: An Analysis of Social Studies Educational Games and Simulations.* Boulder, Colo.: Pruett Press, 1973. Mainly a compilation of analyses in the *Social Studies Curriculum Data Book* and its two supplements, published by the Social Science Education Consortium. Entries are cross-indexed by developer, grade level, subject area, and publisher. Includes, as a bonus, brief descriptions of more than 250 other games and simulations.

Churchill, Richard E., and Churchill, Linda R. *Enriched Social Studies Teaching: Through the Use of Games and Activities.* Palo Alto, Cal.: Fearon Publications, 1973. Useful collection of practical suggestions for classroom activities in the social studies.

Though history is emphasized, many strategies can be used in other areas. Curriculum committees might either recommend the booklet as a resource or use some of the ideas as suggested teaching activities.

Freedman, Miriam, and Paul, Teri. *A Sourcebook for Substitutes and Other Teachers.* Menlo Park, Cal.: Addison-Wesley, 1974. A collection of easy-to-use supplementary activities that have been tested in the classroom. Geared mainly to the secondary level (7-12), these activities emphasize student involvement and can be a big help not only to substitutes who need quick, interesting things to do, but also to regular classroom teachers who value variety and "painless" learning.

Handbook of Simulation Gaming in Social Education, Part II: Directory. University, Ala.: U. of A. Institute of Higher Education Research and Services, 1975. Lists, describes, and comments on more than 700 social studies games. Includes annotated bibliographies and a cross-reference system by subject, grade level, publisher, and cost.

Learning Centers in the Classroom. Washington, D.C.: National Education Association, 1976. Useful little booklet that offers definitions, descriptions of equipment and materials, and numerous suggestions for classroom techniques. Many examples are social studies oriented and may give curriculum committees or teachers a better idea of the learning center approach as an alternative to teacher-dominated, total group operations.

Murphy, Patricia D. *Consumer Education Curriculum Modules: A Spiral-Process Approach.* Washington, D.C.: U.S. Government Printing Office, 1974. Curriculum committees may wish to use this collection of modules either as suggested materials for teachers or for inclusion in the curriculum outline. Of particular value may be the teacher's guides, which provide overview and rationale for each module. The manuals also present field-tested pre- and post-assessment measures.

NCSS How To Do It Packet. Washington, D.C.: National Council for the Social Studies. More than 20 6-8 page pamphlets dealing with specific problems or classroom procedures. Punched for a 3-ring binder. Current titles include:

- **How To Use Oral Reports**
- **How To Conduct a Field Trip**
- **How To Handle Controversial Issues**
- **How To Study a Class**
- **How To Develop Time and Chronological Concepts**
- **How To Teach Library Research Skills in Secondary School Social Studies**
- **How To Ask Questions**
- **How To Use Folksongs**
- **How To Use Simulations**
- **How To Study Political Participation**

Pate, Glenn S., and Parker, Hugh A., Jr. *Designing Classroom Simulations.* Palo Alto, Cal.: Fearon Publications, 1973. Presents rationale for using classroom simulations and shows how to develop "homegrown" simulations in the social studies classroom.

Wagner, Guy, and Gilloley, Laura. *Social Studies Games and Activities: Strengthening Social Studies Skills With Instructional Aids.* Teachers Publishing Corporation, 1971. Contains ideas for more than 100 social studies games and activities for different ability levels in elementary and junior high school grades. Includes classification exercises, dramatizations, and verbal word exercises. Objectives, materials needed, directions, and possible adaptations for the game are described.

Weiland, Thomas P., and Protheroe, Donald W. *Social Science Projects You Can Do.* Englewood Cliffs, N.J.: Prentice-Hall, 1973. Presents a number of useful projects for upper elementary and high school social studies classes. Could serve as an idea book for curriculum committee members or as a valuable reference for social studies teachers or students involved in planning their own program. A sequel by the same authors, *More Social Science Projects You Can Do*, was published by Prentice-Hall in 1974.

Structured Miscellany

No matter how one organizes collections of teaching aids, there are always a number of valuable items that do not fit. Also, in a field such as social studies, there are "hot topics" that appear, find their appropriate spot in the overall curriculum, and then are displaced by a new round of issues, problems, or new developments. Your friendly bibliographers, Miller and Johnson, were faced with "all of the above" in assembling a recommended collection for this publication.

The best title we could think of for the section which follows is "Structured Miscellany." Browse around. See what you can find. Add some more of your own.

Values and Moral Judgments

Duska, Ronald, and Whelan, Mariellen. *Moral Development: A Guide to Piaget and Kohlberg.* New York: Paulist Press, 1975. Thoughtful reading for committees considering the issues of values clarification, moral development, and the like. However, since

the issues discussed are extremely complex, a reading of this text probably should be supplemented with related works by others and/or expert consultants on such matters.

Fraenkel, Jack R. *Helping Students Think and Value: Strategies for Teaching the Social Studies.* Englewood Cliffs, N.J.: Prentice-Hall, 1973. Discusses the nature and use of objectives, subject matter, learning activities, teaching strategies, and evaluation techniques in planning and instruction. Features a wide variety of charts and practical examples for both elementary and secondary level. Of special interest is the final chapter, where the author "gets it all together" in a section on planning.

Galbraith, Ronald E., and Jones, Thomas M. *Moral Reasoning: A Teaching Handbook for Adapting Kohlberg to the Classroom.* Minneapolis: Green Haven Press, 1976. As the title suggests, a practical handbook for using the Kohlberg research approaches in elementary and secondary classrooms. Topics include how to write and present moral dilemma stories, sample dilemmas for classroom use, instructions on how to help students confront moral issues, and a listing of available curriculum materials in this area.

Hall, Robert T., and Davis, John U. *Moral Education in Theory and Practice.* Buffalo: Prometheus, 1975. Presents a background analysis of the philosophical and psychological bases for moral education and values clarification. Includes summaries of the ideas of major theorists in this field, including Lawrence Kohlberg. Also suggests ways in which these ideas may be translated into classroom activities.

Hawley, Robert C. *Value Exploration Through Role-Playing.* New York: Hart, 1974. Presents role-playing techniques appropriate for junior and senior high school classes. Includes eighteen formats for role-playing, and presents a rationale for role-playing as a means to developing moral judgment and making mature decisions.

Mattox, Beverly A. *Getting It Together: Dilemmas for the Classroom Based on Kohlberg's Approach.* San Diego: Pennant Press, 1975. Curriculum committee members may appreciate this explanation of the Kohlberg theory of moral education, which hypothesizes six distinct stages of development—particularly since the Kohlberg theory is becoming increasingly important in structuring of new social studies programs. May also be a useful resource for teachers.

Metcalf, Lawrence E., editor. *Values Education: Rationale, Strategies, and Procedures.* Washington, D.C.: National Council for the Social Studies, 1971. Designed to assist teachers at all levels with problems in values education. Focuses on objectives, teaching strategies, and procedures for values analysis and on resolving values conflicts.

Simon, Sidney B., and Clark, Jay. *Beginning Values Clarification: A Guidebook for the Use of Values Clarification in the Classroom.* San Diego: Pennant Press, 1975. Presents strategies for introducing values clarification to the classroom—that is, helping students understand what things are important to them. Includes thirty-three specific exercises, plus discussions of the values clarification process and rationale for its use.

Simon, Sidney B.; Howe, Leland; and Kirschenbaum, Howard. *Values Clarification: A Handbook of Practical Strategies for Teachers and Students.* New York: Hart, 1972. Contains a collection of seventy-nine strategies and hundreds of suggestions for helping students explore feelings, ideas, and beliefs. May be a handy reference to recommend to teachers who wish to add values clarification lessons to their social studies program.

Superka, Douglas P., et al. *Values Education Sourcebook: Conceptual Approaches, Material Analyses, and an Annotated Bibliography.* Boulder, Colo.: Social Science Education Consortium, 1975. Resource guide that focuses on five major approaches to values clarification, including inculcation, moral development, analysis, clarification, and action learning. Curriculum committees and teachers likely will appreciate the extensive annotated bibliography.

Urban Living

Wisniewski, Richard, editor. *Teaching About Life in the City.* Washington, D.C.: National Council for the Social Studies, 1972. An outline of trends and issues in urban living, focusing on what can be done to alleviate many of the inherent problems. Part One deals with the search for identity in the city. Part Two concerns methods and materials for teaching about city life. Part Three looks with hope at some possibilities for the future.

Wurman, Richard Saul. *Yellow Pages of Learning Resources.* Cambridge, Mass.: MIT Press, 1972. Describes seventy activities that involve use of the city as a learning resource. Organized like the familiar "yellow pages," this book shows how to convert people, places, and processes of the city into learning opportunities. All age groups will find many useful suggestions in this unique format.

Multicultural/Multiethnic

Banks, James A., editor. *Teaching Ethnic Studies: Concepts and Strategies.* Washington, D.C.: National

Council for the Social Studies, 1973. A "no holds barred" treatment of one of the century's most critical educational issues. Included in this yearbook are new conceptual frameworks for ethnic studies, descriptions of promising strategies and materials, and suggestions for dealing with racism in the classroom. Several ethnic minority cultures are featured in individual chapters.

Banks, James A., Chairperson, The NCSS Task Force on Ethnic Studies Curriculum Guidelines. *Curriculum Guidelines for Multiethnic Education.* Washington, D.C.: National Council for the Social Studies, 1976. A position statement that includes a rationale of ethnic pluralism, a set of twenty-three guidelines, and an evaluation checklist with specific items for each general guideline. The focus is on ethnic pluralism rather than cultural pluralism, and the statement is directed to all schools, not just those with mixed ethnic populations.

Gollnick, Donna N.; Klassen, Frank H.; Yff, Joost. *Multicultural Education in the United States: An Analysis and Annotated Bibliography of Selected ERIC Documents.* Washington, D.C.: American Association of Colleges for Teacher Education, 1976. An example of one of many ERIC document summaries that constantly appear. This one, of course, summarized the research and latest ideas presented via papers and reports on ethnic studies and multicultural education in the United States. Curriculum committees should be on the lookout for such collections. The best source usually is a nearby university library with a good education collection.

Scholastic World Cultures Series. Englewood Cliffs, N.J.: Scholastic Book Services, 1970s. A series of up-to-date booklets and filmstrips about various cultures around the world. While these are intended as student materials for classroom use, they can provide insights to a curriculum committee on possible topics and approaches for incorporation into proposed new programs.

Stone, James C., and DeNevi, Donald P., editors. *Teaching Multi-Cultural Populations: Five Heritages.* New York: Van Nostrand Reinhold, 1971. Outstanding collection of readings by noted authors on the Black heritage, the Puerto Rican heritage, the Mexican American heritage, the Indian heritage, and the Asian American heritage in the United States. Curriculum design committees that wish to pay particular attention to the multicultural heritage of American communities will find excellent background material here. This, in turn, can serve as a springboard to readings in applications of approaches that have been successfully tried in other school districts.

Equal Treatment of the Sexes

Sources and the content of guidelines on equal treatment of the sexes change rapidly, but publishers such as McGraw-Hill and Scott Foresman have prepared suggestions for authors, so that sex stereotyping can be avoided. Inasmuch as curriculum committees ultimately are involved in a writing task, members would do well to obtain copies of such guidelines to avoid poisoning their efforts by obvious stereotyping or male-oriented terminology. Other than publishers, committees might contact the Washington office of the National Council for the Social Studies or check with State Departments of Education for similar guidelines and checklists. These also can be used in evaluating materials that may be recommended for inclusion in a local school system curriculum.

Grambs, Jean Dresden, editor. *Teaching About Women in the Social Studies: Concepts, Methods, and Materials.* Washington, D.C.: National Council for the Social Studies, 1976. A resource bulletin—rather than a curriculum guide—for teachers who want to present women fairly in social studies classes. Critical concepts and issues are presented, under each topic, and guidance is provided for the selection of content and materials. The emphasis throughout this bulletin is on practical aspects of subject matter presentation.

The National Education Association, which counts several hundred thousand professional women among its membership, also has packets of information on sex-role stereotyping.

Finale: Keeping Up with the Projects

The 1960s and early 1970s saw the completion of a number of significant curriculum projects in the social studies. Some of them have faded away, for one reason or another, but others have become a mainstay of revised curricula in many communities around the country.

Also, as the major publishers of social studies materials have revised or developed new text series, they frequently have incorporated the best elements from various projects. Examination of the advertisements in *Social Education* reveals series that are focused on basic concepts and understandings of the social science disciplines that contribute content for the social studies curriculum. They also recommend many of the special techniques extensively tried and confirmed by action research in the late 1960s and early 1970s.

Many of the new series represent investments of millions of dollars on the part of the developer-publishers. They are multimedia in orientation, provide for heavy learner involvement, make some attempt to include material of interest to multi-ethnic and diverse student populations, and furnish extensive help to the teacher who is interested in trying new classroom strategies. Publishers, in many cases, have moved from a single, hardbound textbook to collections of pamphlets, maps, slide-tape sets, and other materials that can be used in a variety of sequences. Curriculum committees that would want to follow a complete pre-packaged program may choose items from several publishers, and meld them together into a sequence that will fit local needs.

Obviously, school districts that get into multimedia, multisource programs must anticipate the need for a support system. This should include persons who can write bridging materials, establish and run workshops for teachers, and provide regular supervisory or resource assistance to school-level personnel.

While the 1965 predecessor of this publication, *Social Studies Curriculum Improvement: A Guide for Local Committees* (NCSS), carried several pages of listings on "post-Sputnik" projects, the situation has changed somewhat. Instead, we recommend that you consult some of the sources cited earlier in this chapter, and follow up with a review of publishers' notices and current issues of *Social Education*. In February, 1975, for example, Irving Morrissett authored an article which summarized user ratings of twenty-four projects. Another excellent source is the *Social Studies Curriculum Materials Data Book* from the Social Science Education Consortium in Boulder, Colorado.

Index

110

Index of Schools, Programs, and Associations

Adult Performance Level Project, 47, 49–51, 58
American Association of University Women, 28
American Council of Learned Societies, 93
American Society for Curriculum and Development, 98, 99
American Sociological Association, 91
Anthropology Curriculum Study Project, 27
Asian Studies Center, 23
Association of American Geographers, 91

Center of Syracuse University, 23
Center on History, Amherst College, 23
Columbus in the World/The World in Columbus (Ohio) Project, 52
Curriculum Information Network, 98

Development Economic Education Program (DEEP), 42, 43, 47, 58

Educational Resources Information Center, 98, 99
Educational Services, Inc., 23
Esperanza Model, 52, 53, 59

Father Organization of Los Angeles City Unified School District, 56
Ford Foundation, 20
Foxfire Project, 47, 48, 58

Georgia, University of, social studies program, 23
Greater Cleveland Council of the Social Studies, 27

Harvard University Project, 23
Head Start, 55

Illinois, University of, social studies program, 23
Industrial Relations Center, 27
Institute on Political and Legal Education (IPLE) Project of New Jersey, 37

John Hay Fellowship Program, 21, 27
Joint Council on Economic Education, 23, 42, 47, 58

Lakewood High School, 27
League of Women Voters, 28
Lincoln Filene Center for Citizenship and Public Affairs at Tufts University, 27
Loblolly Project, 48

Mansfield City Schools, 17–40
Mansfield Program, 23
Mansfield Senior High School, 19
Mansfield Ohio State University Campus, 36
Mayor's Committee on Human Relations, 28
Mendocino College Interdisciplinary Education Project, 47, 48–49, 58
Mid-America program, 52
Minnesota, University of, social studies program, 23

National Assessment of Educational Progress Program, 88
NCA Foreign Relations Project, 27
National Council for the Social Studies, 7, 13, 43, 86, 93, 98, 99, 102, 108
New York, State of, curriculum guidelines of, 43

Parent Involvement component of Project Follow Through, 52–53
Parent-Teacher Association Council, 28
Parma High School (Ohio), 27
Pennsylvania Curriculum Center, 23
Peoria and the World Project, 47, 51–52, 58
President's Committee on Consumer Interests, 101
Project Follow Through, 52–53, 55–56, 59

Rabun Gap (Georgia) High School, 48
Richland County Chapter of the Ohio Genealogical Society, 23, 28
Richland County Historical Society, 23, 28

San Francisco State College Center, 23
Social Science Education Consortium, 44, 98, 101–02, 109
Social Studies Curriculum Center, Carnegie-Mellon University, 27
Social Studies Curriculum Review Committee, 36, 37
Social Studies Development Center, Indiana University, 51
Social Studies Field Agent Training Program, Indiana University, 43, 46, 59
Sociological Resources for Secondary Schools, University of Michigan, 23

Title III ESEA Project, 31–32
Title III NDEA Conference, 27
Tri-County Goal Development Project, 91
Twin Cities Social Studies Service Center, 42, 43, 46–47, 58

United States Office of Education, 56
Urban-Rural Development Program, 53, 56–57, 59

West Islip Social Studies Program, 42, 43–46, 58

Subject-Matter Index

Accountability, 80 89–90.
Administrators, role of, 7, 15, 18, 29, 40, 42; and curriculum change, 20, 22, 37–38, 81.
Articulation, program, 18, 37
Assessment. *See* Evaluation
Attitudes, 20, 22, 31
"Bargain prices," 11–14, 45. *See also*, Funding
Behavioral objectives, 8, 11–12, 90, 95. *See also*, Evaluation
Board of Education, 8, 34, 44, 45, 70; and curriculum change, 21, 22, 37–38
Career education, 11, 38, 35, 73
Caring, necessity of, 4, 6, 9, 11–12, 57, 66
Change, 4, 5, 25, 31, 46, 65, 74
Children, development of, 4, 41, 70, 73, 74, 82, 86

Index of Titles

Index prepared by Mary W. Matthews
Book design and production by Joseph Perez
Typography by Byrd PrePress
Printing and binding by Waverly Press